D1451344

HEALTHIER Gluten-Free

HEALTHIER
Gluten-Free

All-Natural, Whole-Grain Recipes Made with Healthy Ingredients and Zero Fillers

Lisa Howard

RM237.86.H685 2014
Howard, Lisa, 1977- author.
Healthier gluten-free :
all-natural, whole-grain
recipes made with healthy
ingredients and zero fillers
Beverly, MA : Fair Winds

Fair Winds Press
100 Cummings Center, Suite 406L
Beverly, MA 01915

fairwindspress.com • quarryspoon.com

©2014 Fair Winds Press
Text ©2014 Lisa Howard
Photography ©2014 Kate Lewis

First published in the USA in 2014 by
Fair Winds Press, a member of
Quarto Publishing Group USA Inc.
100 Cummings Center
Suite 406-L
Beverly, MA 01915-6101
www.fairwindspress.com
Visit www.QuarrySPOON.com and help us celebrate food and culture one spoonful at a time!

18 17 16 15 14   1 2 3 4 5

ISBN: 978-1-59233-598-5

Digital edition published in 2014
eISBN: 978-1-62788-016-9

Library of Congress Cataloging-in-Publication Data

Howard, Lisa, 1977- author.
  Healthier gluten-free : all-natural, whole-grain recipes that get rid of the refined starches, fillers, and chemical gums for a truly healthy gluten-free diet / Lisa Howard.
      pages cm
  1. Gluten-free diet--Recipes. 2. Cooking (Cereals) 3. Grain. 4. Natural foods. I. Title.
  RM237.86.H685 2014
  641.3′31--dc23
                    2013048704

Cover and book design by Caitlin Keegan
Photography/Food Styling by Kate Lewis
Prop Styling by Maryellen Echle
Printed and bound in China

The information in this book is for educational purposes only. It is not intended to replace the advice of a physician or medical practitioner. Please see your health care provider before beginning any new health program.

To my mom, the best friend I'll ever have and the most talented cook I know.

Contents

INTRODUCTION

Welcome to a happier, healthier, gluten-free life! With so many gluten-free ingredients available in grocery stores and more gluten-free dishes on restaurant menus, going gluten-free is a lot easier than it used to be. Heck, with an open mind and this book in hand, it will be a culinary adventure! Time to awaken your taste buds to new flavors, and the rest of you to improved health. Here's to whole-grain, gluten-free deliciousness!

You'll especially love this book if you:

- Must avoid gluten and/or wheat because of celiac disease, gluten intolerance/sensitivity, or a wheat allergy, but want to do it right and in the healthiest way possible.

- Are thinking about avoiding gluten because you or someone you know suffers from arthritis, ADD, autism, depression, diabetes, fibromyalgia, IBS, migraines, thyroid disease, or any of the more than 50 auto-immune disorders that have been associated with celiac disease and gluten intolerance/sensitivity.

- Have no problem with gluten but are curious about what other grains—and seeds and nuts and legumes and roots—have to offer.

- Are diabetic, overweight, and/or suffering from metabolic syndrome and need to adopt a whole-grain lifestyle.

- Would like more variety on your plate.

- Would like to enjoy whole-grain, whole-food dishes and baked goods made without refined sugar.

- Would like to learn more about baking and cooking elements so that you can create your own whole-grain, whole-food recipes.

- Are thinking about switching to pastured animal products and natural fats.

Knowledge is power! And knowledge makes things less scary, too. If you're feeling intimidated by the whole "gluten thing," don't be—you're about to find out what gluten actually is, how it may be affecting you, and where (and where not) you'll find it. You're about to become an expert!

Chapter 1 | Defining Gluten in Everyday Terms

WHAT GLUTEN IS

Ever played with Play-Doh? That's gluten. You can "make" gluten yourself by simply stirring cold water and all-purpose white flour together in a bowl until it begins to turn into a thick paste. Eventually, the dough becomes firm enough to pick up and knead. That's gluten. If you mix it with dye and give it to a child to play with, it's Play-Doh. In Asian, vegan, and macrobiotic cuisines, hunks of gluten are called "seitan" or "wheat meat" because it's commonly served in place of meat.

On a little less fun and a little more fundamental level, gluten consists of two proteins—gliadin and glutenin—woven together into a stretchy network. The elasticity of that network is what allows bakers to create an infinite variety of airy, chewy breads. French baguettes are one of the best examples of how stubbornly elastic gluten is. Ever tried playing tug-of-war with a loaf? Your arms might give out before the loaf does.

WHERE GLUTEN IS

While several grains contain gluten, wheat contains by far the most: More than 80 percent of wheat's inner starchy endosperm is composed of gluten. That high gluten content makes wheat the ideal grain to use when making yeast-risen doughs and breads. Gluten is also imperative for doughs that have to be stretched paper-thin, like the puff pastry dough used in baklava and croissants.

You'll find wheat occupying grocery shelves in many different forms. Durum (sometimes also called emmer) and semolina are both used to make pasta; bulgur is coarsely chopped durum wheat. Couscous is made from semolina. Graham flour and matzo dough are made of various types of wheat. And as mentioned earlier, seitan is unabashed, flat-out gluten.

Then there are wheat's gluten-containing cohorts: barley, rye, kamut, spelt, farro, and triticale. While some people who cannot eat wheat can safely consume barley and rye, those who cannot eat gluten cannot eat any gluten-containing grains or the products mentioned above.

And did you know that different kinds of wheat flour contain different levels of gluten? For example, while flour made of hard winter wheat—commonly known as "bread flour"—contains about 14 percent gluten, "cake flour," made from soft winter wheat, contains only about 7 percent gluten. As the term *soft* implies, this flour is used to make cakes, muffins, pies, and biscuits with soft, crumbly textures rather than chewy baked goods like those French baguettes we talked about earlier. That's good to know, because low-gluten favorites can easily become gluten-free favorites, with no one the wiser!

WHEAT & ITS MANY NAMES

Following are some of the many varieties and names of wheat:

• Semolina	• All-purpose flour	• Emmer
• Durum	• Self-rising flour	• Farro
• Bulgur	• Cake flour	• Einkorn
• Couscous	• Farina	• Triticale
• Pastas	• Pastry flour	• Dinkel
• Bread flour	• Spelt	
• Bleached flour	• Kamut	

It's important to point out that *glutenous* does not mean the same thing as *glutinous*. *Glutenous* means "gluten-containing," while *glutinous* means "sticky," as in glutinous (sticky) rice. While it's possible to be glutenous and glutinous at the same time—think of that childhood Play-Doh—"glutinous rice" and "glutinous rice flour" are in fact gluten-free (as are foods made with them, as long as no gluten-containing ingredients have been added).

These two non-wheat grains also contain gluten:

- Rye
- Barley

Just avoiding "wheat" means avoiding everything included in the first list, while avoiding "gluten" means avoiding all the foods from both lists. Remember, all wheat contains gluten, but gluten is found in more than just wheat.

WHAT ABOUT OATS?

Oats are a gray area in the gluten world. While they don't have the same set of proteins that form gluten in other grains, oats are usually grown in or near wheat fields, are processed alongside or with wheat, and are made into products that also contain wheat. The good news is that some producers and manufacturers are starting to offer gluten-free oats, meaning those grown and processed apart from wheat, barley, and other glutenous grains, so keep an eye out for those "safe" versions.

SECTION HIGHLIGHTS

Wheat goes by many different names, including semolina, durum, bulgur, couscous, and farina.

Other grains besides wheat contain gluten, the most common ones being barley, rye, triticale, spelt, kamut, emmer, farro, and contaminated oats.

Oats do not naturally contain the type of gluten found in wheat, but oats are often cross-contaminated by wheat and other gluten-containing grains. That's why it's important to seek out oats labeled "gluten-free."

Traditional low-gluten baked goods can easily be made into gluten-free baked goods.

CHAPTER 2 | GLUTEN & YOU

A Timeline of Celiac Disease

HOW DOES GLUTEN AFFECT US?

More and more, people are discovering that they are sensitive, intolerant, or allergic to certain foods, particularly wheat and gluten. Celiac disease in particular is an autoimmune disorder directly connected to gluten, in which the gluten proteins inflame and damage the villi in the small intestine, making it impossible for them to do their job. Because the villi play an essential role in the body's ability to absorb nutrients from all food, if a celiac continues to consume gluten, it becomes difficult for the body to absorb and reap the benefits from any food, not just those that contain gluten.

Although physicians have been describing the symptoms of celiac disease since 100 C.E., doctors weren't able to officially name and define the disease until the 1880s. In 1921, a British physician came up with a milk-and-protein diet for celiacs that proved to be successful; fifteen years later, a Dutch doctor realized that the cause of celiacs' woes was cereal grains. The slim tube used to conduct intestinal biopsies to verify cases of celiac disease was invented in 1955 and is still in use today. Being able to definitively assess the damage caused by celiac disease sparked a new era of research.

According to www.celiac.com, even with advanced screening procedures, doctors in 1990 thought only forty thousand Americans had celiac disease. That estimate tripled by the turn of the century. The National Institutes of Health now estimates that about 1 percent of the U.S. population—or about three million Americans—suffer from celiac disease. It also affects large numbers of people in Ireland (estimated at one in three hundred) and Finland (estimates are as high as one in one hundred).

When a person doesn't have celiac disease but does have a wheat allergy, ingesting wheat can trigger immediate, obvious reactions (like difficulty in breathing) as well as less-severe ones (like itchy, watery eyes). Both celiacs and wheat-allergic people have to be very careful—the former to avoid all gluten-containing grains and the latter to avoid wheat.

Those who are intolerant or sensitive to gluten usually find it in their best interests to avoid gluten due to the debilitating, problematic, or flat-out uncomfortable reactions they experience when they eat gluten. That could mean anything from a pounding headache to an upset stomach to a very urgent need to find a bathroom. In short, many people would rather feel their best at all times, and often that means embracing a gluten-free lifestyle.

WHY SO MANY PROBLEMS WITH GLUTEN?

So why the sudden increase in food-related discomforts and diseases? For one, because of the sharp increase in the number of fortified, enriched, and processed foods on grocery store shelves. "Fortified" foods are foods that contain nutrients or ingredients that normally wouldn't be found in that food, like the calcium that's added to orange juice. "Enriched" foods are foods that have had a crucial ingredient removed and then partially put back, like "enriched" white flour. These foods are highly processed. We'll talk more about enriched foods in Part II.

The problem with fortified and processed foods is that it's easy to wind up eating far more of the same ingredient—wheat being a prime example—than we're equipped to handle. Most foods that make up the American diet today wouldn't be possible to create without a disproportionate reliance on wheat and industrial-scale processing techniques. And because neither of these things has been around long enough for our bodies to adapt to them, we're finding that such foods interfere with how our bodies operate (and how well they operate) on a day-to-day basis.

Wheat/gluten is a prime example of too-much-of-the-same-thing fortification: Many already-high-in-gluten breads have extra gluten added to them to increase their elastic characteristics and protein content—and this is in addition to being crossbred and engineered to have a higher natural gluten content. Protein bars, protein powders, multi-grain baked goods and cereals, and other protein-fortified foods also often contain added gluten in the form of wheat starch or wheat germ.

Our reliance on refined white flour rather than whole wheat flour also adds more gluten to our diets. That's because while whole wheat flour contains the endosperm, the bran, and the germ, refined flour only contains the gluten-rich endosperm, making it proportionately higher in gluten. When it comes to food, at least, the older generation is certainly justified in saying that things "just aren't the way they used to be"!

A final piece of the puzzle in explaining the recent upsurge in food-related maladies is that medical science has gotten better at diagnosing conditions like celiac disease and food allergies. Public awareness surrounding these food issues has also increased.

As our understanding of these conditions and their causes continues to grow, we may soon see that the solution lies in embracing (and enjoying!) a variety of minimally processed, whole-grain foods, particularly dishes that don't rely on wheat.

FINDING FOOD YOU CAN EAT

In general, the more processed a food is and the more ingredients it contains, the more likely it is to contain gluten. Your best bet is to stick to the basics: Unadorned fruits and vegetables are gluten-free, as are simple dairy products like milk, plain yogurt, butter, and eggs still in their shells. Many whole grains and flours made from those grains are also gluten-free provided that you purchase them individually rather than as part of a preblended mix. (See "Gluten-Free Flour Families" on page 21 for more information on gluten-free grains.) Unmarinated/unprocessed meats and seafood are also gluten-free. Spices and herbs—though not always premade mixes—are gluten-free, as are oils. Vinegar is gluten-free, with the exception of malt vinegar, which is made from barley.

Stick to whole-food basics, avoid the center grocery aisles where most of the processed foods lurk, and you'll have endless gluten-free options.

Gluten-Related Problems

The following are common ailments listed as "associated diseases and disorders" on www.celiac.com. If you suffer from any of these conditions, adopting a gluten-free lifestyle may help alleviate or eliminate symptoms caused by these chronic diseases. Going gluten-free can't hurt you, but it can really help!

- Arthritis
- Attention deficit disorder (ADD)
- Autism
- Chronic fatigue syndrome (CFS)
- Crohn's disease
- Diabetes
- Fibromyalgia
- Infertility issues
- Irritable bowel syndrome (IBS)
- Migraines
- Multiple sclerosis (MS)
- Osteoporosis
- Psoriasis
- Thyroid disorders

HIDDEN GLUTEN

Following is a short list of not-so-obvious foods that may—or may not—include gluten. Remember to read ingredient labels carefully!

BEER. Most beer is brewed with wheat or barley, although more and more gluten-free beers are becoming available—these beers are brewed with rice, corn, sorghum, and/or buckwheat and are labeled "gluten-free."

CEREAL. The good news is you can make your own gluten-free cereal in fewer than ten minutes, and it'll taste ten times better than store-bought cereal!

PREPARED AND PACKAGED FOODS. These include canned baked beans, canned fruit fillings, gravies/sauces, and vegetables with prepared sauces.

SOY SAUCE. Look for wheat-free tamari instead.

SALAD DRESSINGS. Dressings are disturbingly full of additives, but it's easy to make your own dressing by drizzling oil and vinegar/citrus juice over your salads.

BROTHS, STOCKS, AND SOUPS. Look for simple, organic versions made from basic ingredients and always read the ingredient label with an attentive eye.

MALTED FOODS AND MALTED MILK. Malted ingredients are generally made with gluten-containing barley, although the malt used to make gluten-free beer is typically made of sorghum, rice, or millet. Steer clear of any malted ingredient that is not labeled as being gluten-free.

STORE-BOUGHT DESSERTS. These include commercial custards, ice creams, and puddings.

PROCESSED MEATS. These include hot dogs and deli cuts.

CHEWING GUM AND BREATH MINTS.

ANYTHING WITH UNRECOGNIZABLE INGREDIENTS. These include fillers, stabilizers, thickeners, starches, natural flavors, modified food starch, MSG, emulsifiers, and binders.

Most Common Food Allergens

The American Academy of Allergy, Asthma, and Immunology esti- mates that twelve million Americans suffer from a food allergy. Almost 90 percent of those allergies are caused by one or more of these eight most common allergens:

- Cow's milk
- Eggs
- Fish
- Peanuts (which are actually legumes, not nuts—they grow underground)
- Shellfish
- Soy
- Tree nuts (which grow on trees: almonds, walnuts, pecans, hazelnuts, etc.)
- Wheat

Because these eight allergens cause so many reactions, the Food Aller- gen Labeling and Consumer Protection Act of 2004 mandates that these eight ingredients must be clearly listed on food labels. That's helpful for anyone trying to avoid those eight particular foods. That said, while wheat and ingredients cross-contaminated by wheat must be listed on food labels, "gluten" is not on the list of official allergens, and as we've learned, gluten can be found in other non-wheat foods, including barley and rye. Therefore, anyone who must avoid gluten must either search for foods marked "gluten-free" or read ingredient lists with an attentive eye to verify that the food in question does not include a gluten-containing ingredient. Buyer, please beware!

There are differences be- tween having celiac disease (cannot eat gluten), having a wheat allergy (cannot eat wheat but may be able to eat other gluten-containing grains, such as barley and rye), and having a gluten intolerance/sensitivity (eat- ing gluten probably makes you feel unwell). Under- standing where you are on this spectrum is important in setting up a diet that works best for you.

Several factors explain the rise in gluten issues in our population. One is the amount of wheat and other additives being unneces- sarily added to our foods through artificial process- ing. Another is the rise in awareness and proper diagnosis.

Gluten can pop up in unex- pected places, so becoming a label-reading expert is important!

Ever wondered what "whole-grain" really means? Or what all the whole-grain fuss is about? Keep reading—focusing on whole-grain cooking and baking is especially important for gluten-free folks. (Good thing we have so many whole-grain flours to choose from!) You'll also learn about key ingredients such as dairy products, unrefined oils, and natural sweeteners, and you'll see how to transform your newfound knowledge into your newly delicious day-to-day life.

CHAPTER 3 | THE IMPORTANCE OF WHOLE-GRAIN AND GLUTEN-FREE

A BRIEF HISTORY OF FLOURS AND MILLING
Long before millers knew how to bleach and bromate, people ate all kinds of grains. The grains were eaten as a whole "three-for-one" package deal, if you will: the hard outer bran, the inner oil-rich germ, and the inner starchy endosperm. Whole grains were tremendously useful as a food source because they could be stored for months or even years in their unadulterated state.

These grains were pounded into coarse flours that were made into flatbreads, dense cakes, mashes, porridges, and more. Prompt use of the whole-grain flour was—and is—key, because once grains are broken apart and their innards exposed to air, the oils contained in the germ begin to go rancid and the nutritional value and flavor of the grain begins to dwindle if not used quickly.

HOW REFINEMENT BEGAN
Flour began to be widely consumed when ancient Greeks and Romans developed mills to process their grains into flour. Gradually, the millstones used for grinding went from being human- and animal-powered to being powered by watermills and windmills. In the late 1800s, traditional millstones were replaced by metal rollers capable of crushing grain into refined powder.

Unfortunately, this technology came at a price: The more efficient the milling methods became, the less nutrient-dense the flour became. Millers realized it was more profitable to separate the bran and germ from the endosperm because the delicate oils are present in the germ and not the starchy endosperm. As a result, flour made strictly from the endosperm, they found, lasted far longer than flour made from whole grains, making it easier to store and transport. Such flour also had a milder flavor and resulted in lighter-textured baked goods. It was a smart business decision, but not necessarily smart for health.

In the case of wheat, the ability to refine the flour into endosperm-only flour (what we now call "all-purpose" flour) also meant that the resulting flour had a higher gluten content because gluten proteins are found mainly in the endosperm. This refined flour gave birth to most of the baked goods we know today, from chewy baguettes to flaky pastries. But the process wasn't limited to only wheat: The same refinement began to be used on rice and corn, too.

THE IMPACT OF REFINED FLOURS
By the early 1900s, the nutritional pitfalls of refined wheat flour, degerminated cornmeal, and polished white rice had become too great to ignore: Pellagra was rampant in the American South, and beriberi was sending people in Asia to premature graves. Both were diseases that resulted from vitamin B deficiencies, a deficiency that gained ground as vitamin B–rich germs in grains were more and more aggressively milled out. Fortunately, nutrition research throughout the 1920s and '30s revealed the existence of those B vitamins and where they were to be found, and solutions were enacted to deal with the deficiencies. The 1940s saw the voluntary "enrichment" of flour as manufacturers replaced some of what had been taken out: thiamine (B_1), niacin (B_3), riboflavin (B_2), and folic acid (B_9). That's why you see those vitamins listed on "enriched" products.

"Great!" you're probably thinking. "That fixes things, then."

Not really. Saying that stripped-out flours are "enriched" is like saying that you've been enriched after a thief has stolen fifty dollars from you and then handed back ten dollars. You're still short forty dollars!

"Robbed" would be a more appropriate term for both the human and the grain victim. Not only is the grain still missing some B vitamins, it's missing the vast majority of its fiber, fats (including the essential omegas), minerals, protein, and other vitamins. The endosperm is mostly starch, and while that starch is a ready source of energy for a sprouting seed, humans need much more than straight starch to satisfy our dietary needs. Excessive consumption of straight starch contributes and/or leads to conditions such as diabetes, impaired digestion, impaired immune system functions, and many other chronic ailments. Understanding what makes for a healthy foodstyle comes down to common sense: Humans evolved to run on whole grains, not processed ones, and if we try to subsist on a stripped-out, starchy grain diet, our bodies become prone to disease.

From a culinary standpoint, refined grains also get failing marks in the flavor department—one bland refined grain tastes pretty much like another. In comparison, when it comes to whole grains, there's a wide spectrum of flavors to savor: nutty, earthy, creamy, sharp, smooth . . . the list goes on and on, especially if you include non-grain flours. "Flour," after all, refers to any dry, edible powder.

COMPARING WHOLE GRAINS TO REFINED GRAINS

No matter which foodstyle you follow—vegetarian, flexitarian, omnivorous—you're better off eating whole grains rather than refined ones. This is one of the few core principles of nutritional science that is not hotly debated. But despite widespread acceptance of the "whole-grain-is-better" principle, most commercially baked goods and home-baked goods continue to be made with refined, nutritionally deficient flours. This is true for gluten-free products, too.

As I've mentioned, a big part of the reason why refined wheat flour is so popular is that it provides more gluten and therefore more elasticity, spring, and softness. Plus, refined-flour products mean higher profit margins because they're less susceptible to mold and rancidity than whole-grain products, whether we're talking about gluten-free or wheat-based ones.

As an example, let's take a quick look at the ingredient labels of some gluten-free products to see how they score in the whole-grain/not-so-whole-grain department:

Glutino Multi-Grain Cracker ingredients: Cornstarch, white rice flour, organic palm oil, modified cornstarch, dextrose, liquid whole eggs, yeast, salt, fennel seeds, poppy seeds, guar gum, ammonium bicarbonate, sodium bicarbonate, mono and diglycerides, natural flavor.
Analysis: Yes, these crackers are technically "multigrain," but unfortunately those grains—corn and rice—are not in their whole forms. Instead, we have cornstarch and white rice flour. The whole-grain alternatives would be corn flour and brown rice flour.

Udi's Gluten-Free Whole-Grain Bread ingredients: Water, tapioca starch, brown rice flour, potato starch, canola oil, egg whites, sugar, teff flour, flaxseed meal, yeast, xanthan gum, apple cider vinegar, salt, baking powder, cultured dextrose, ascorbic acid, enzymes.
Analysis: Again, while this bread does feature some whole grains—brown rice flour, teff flour, and flaxseed meal—the first and third main flours used are starches (tapioca starch and potato starch). Bread that's 100 percent whole-grain would use potato flour and various whole grains/foods in lieu of starches.

And now let's compare refined flours to whole-grain flours directly to get a better idea of the differences. Pretty impressive, isn't it?

Grain (Starches vs. Whole Flour)	Calories	Carbohy-drates (grams)	Fiber (grams)	Protein (grams)	Vitamin A (% Daily Value)	Vitamin C (% Daily Value)	Iron (% Daily Value)
White rice flour (a starch), ¼ cup	150	32	1	2	-	-	-
Brown rice flour (a whole grain), ¼ cup	140	31	2	3	-	-	4%
Whole-grain flours contain **more fiber and protein** than do refined flours.							
Cornstarch (a starch), ¼ cup	120	28	-	-	-	-	-
Corn flour (a whole grain), ¼ cup	110	22	4	2	1%	-	3%
Whole-grain flours also contain **fewer carbohydrates** than do refined flours.							
Potato starch (a starch), 3 tablespoons	120	30	-	-	-	-	-
Potato flour (a whole food), 3 tablespoons	120	27	2	3	-	10%	35%
Whole-grain flours also contain **more minerals and vitamins** than do refined flours.							

AN EASY SOLUTION: GRIND YOUR OWN FLOUR!

Luckily, there's an easy way to access incredibly fresh, nutrient-rich, whole-food flours (and save money, too): your coffee/spice grinder. If you don't have one, visit your nearest home goods store and check out the small appliances section. A coffee/spice grinder is the best tool you can have in a whole-grain kitchen! And because coffee/spice grinders are typically the least-expensive member of the kitchen gadget pack, your small investment will be well, well worth it.

You'll save time because it only takes about ten seconds to grind soft nuts, seeds, and grains into flour, and you'll save money because you can purchase a single bag of whole grains and then use them as grains in one dish and freshly ground flour in another. Who doesn't like a two-for-one deal?

We'll talk more about grinding your own flour in Chapter 5: Core Concepts of Gluten-Free Baking (page 35), and you'll find tips for grinding and using your own flour in several recipes throughout the book.

SECTION HIGHLIGHTS

Whole grains retain their nutritional value and flavor far longer than milled flours do.

Refined, "enriched" flour is still missing most of its original (and important!) nutrients.

Humans cannot be healthy on a diet of refined foods—whole foods are our natural fuel.

Most baked goods—both gluten-free and wheat-based—are not whole-grain.

Grinding your own flour in a coffee/spice grinder only takes about ten seconds, and doing so will allow you to enjoy the freshest, most nutrient-packed flour while also saving you money and improving your health (plus, home-ground flour just tastes better!).

CHAPTER 4 | MAKING HEALTHY WHOLE-FOOD CHOICES

WHOLE GRAINS, FLOURS, AND FOODS: THE SMART CHOICE

Now that you've learned about whole grains and why they're so important for everybody—especially gluten-free folks who want to get their health back on track—let's take a look at gluten-free flours and other core food groups, including dairy products, eggs, oils, and sweeteners. Like grains, these products need to be selected carefully and always offer the best nutrition in their fresh, whole-food forms. No need to settle for processed, refined ingredients when you can enjoy tastier, better-for-you real foods with minimal time and effort—and a big payoff for your health!

GLUTEN-FREE FLOUR FAMILIES

For the sake of exploring all of our more than thirty gluten-free flour options in an organized way, let's first group our flours into families: grain flours, nut flours, seed flours, legume flours, root/tuber/starch flours, and miscellaneous. Let's also define "flour" as simply a fine, soft powder.

Within these main categories of flours—which we'll discuss one at a time—you'll find that while each flour has its own unique characteristics, collectively, flours in the same family have a similar flavor and purpose.

Some of the flours you're about to meet are not commonly found in the United States (but are well known in other countries), some are regional U.S. specialties, and others have fallen out of favor. Most of these flours, however, are available through online specialty retailers, and many are also available in health-food/natural-food stores. Some mainstream grocers are even starting to feature a wider selection of flours—check the baking aisle, the grains aisle, and the gluten-free aisle to see what's available. And don't forget that many flours are easy and inexpensive to make at home! If a nut, seed, or grain is hard enough and dry enough to be ground rather than puréed, it can become flour. For example, raw almonds are dry enough to grind, but raw pecans turn into nut butter. But once you toast the pecans—therefore drying them out a little—they can be ground into flour, too.

If you're buying flour at the store, make sure your flour has not been blended with other flours. Cross-contamination can also occur when flours are milled on shared equipment or when bulk bins are not kept strictly gluten-free. For very sensitive individuals, this can be a major problem; for others, it may not be a concern. And of course, you and your health professional need to evaluate where you stand on the oats issue.

GRAIN FLOURS

Because whole grains still contain their oil-rich germs, whole-grain flours should be stored in the refrigerator to prolong their flavor and nutrition. Cooked whole grains can be refrigerated for one week. They make great breakfast cereals!

GRAIN/FLOUR	TASTE & BEST USE
Corn (cornmeal, corn flour, hominy, grits, polenta, etc.)	Stone-ground cornmeal is particularly rich and buttery and makes deliciously chewy breads and muffins. Corn flour makes a mellow backdrop for both sweet and savory dishes.
Millet	Millet tastes and looks like couscous and makes wonderful pilafs and grain salads; millet flour is faintly nutty and blends well with other flours.

(continued)

(continued from previous page)

Grain/Flour	Taste & Best Use
Sorghum	A slightly sweet and nutty grain, sorghum flour is perfect for cakes, cookies, and other sweets.
Teff	This tiny, dark, nutty African staple grain makes fantastic porridges. It can easily be ground into a flour and used to make flavorful cookies, biscotti, bread . . . anything, really.
Oats (certified gluten-free)	Steel-cut oats are ideal as cereal, in soups and stews, and in cookies. Oat flour gives a hearty, chewy character to everything from crusts to pancakes; rolled oats make tasty granola when combined with nuts and dried fruits.

Nut Flours

Like grains, most nuts are rich in oils and should also be refrigerated. If you want to make an ultra-nutty treat, use nut flour and chopped or whole nuts in your baked goods.

Nut/Flour	Taste & Best Use
Almond	Almonds are dry enough to be ground into flour, yet oily enough to impart a distinctive moist flavor to baked goods. Freshly ground almond flour is much more moist and flavorful than store-bought almond flour and is simple to make at home. (*Meal* and *flour* are nearly interchangeable terms, by the way—meal is simply coarsely ground flour.) It's easiest to make almond flour from unblanched sliced almonds that still have traces of their papery skins clinging to their edges. The skins provide more fiber, flavor, and color.
Hazelnut	Because hazelnuts are much harder than almonds, they may need to be chopped before being ground into flour. The flour makes for a flavorful addition to cookies, muffins, cakes, and crusts.
Peanut	Technically, peanuts are legumes, not nuts, but their overridingly nutty flavor and high-protein profile make their flour a welcome presence in everything from pancakes to breads.
Chestnut	Because chestnuts have more starch and less oil than all other nuts, they behave like a traditional grain flour. You can often use chestnut flour as the only flour when baking.
Brazil nut	Brazil nuts have to be chopped before being ground into a very moist and rich flour. Swapping out as little as ¼ cup of flour for ¼ cup of Brazil nut flour can give a recipe an amazing texture and flavor.
Toasted walnuts, pecans, and pine nuts	While these nuts are often too oily to be ground into flour when they're raw, if you dry-toast them in a skillet over medium-low heat for about 5 minutes, you can let them cool and then grind them into flour with a few quick bursts of your grinder or food processor. They'll add new dimensions to your baked goods!

Nut/Flour	Taste & Best Use
Acorn nut	Koreans, Japanese, and Native Americans have traditionally processed acorns into flour used to make everything from noodles to cakes.

Seed Flours

Some seeds are treated like nuts; others are thought of as grains. Either way, refrigerate your seed flours and enjoy their distinct flavors in a variety of culinary settings.

Seed/Flour	Taste & Best Use
Amaranth	These tiny, crunchy South American seeds are faintly bitter and pair well with savory baked goods and dishes.
Buckwheat	An unfortunately named plant, buckwheat has nothing to do with wheat—it's related to rhubarb. Toasted buckwheat flour (kasha) has a very earthy, full, almost bitter taste that's perfect for savory crepes and Russian-style blinis. Whole, raw buckwheat groats and the flour made from them are much milder.
Quinoa	Another South American seed, quinoa is nuttier than amaranth. When you cook whole quinoa seeds, they begin to unravel and their hulls form enchanting little curlicues. Quinoa flour has a grassy, delicate flavor.
Flax	Not only do freshly ground flaxseeds add a nutty character to smoothies, but they also act as natural thickening agents in baked goods, and can even be used as an egg replacer.
Chia	Much like flaxseeds, chia seeds will thicken liquids and batters, helping them stick together. Chia has a much milder flavor than flax; it's reminiscent of poppy seeds. Like flax, chia can be used as an egg replacer.
Poppy	We're used to using poppy seeds as a garnish for bagels, but Russian and East European recipes make liberal use of freshly ground poppy seeds. They make a luscious, flavorful flour!
Sesame	Raw sesame seeds can be ground into butter/tahini, but toasted sesame seeds can be ground into flour and used to make unbelievably rich crackers and other savory baked goods.
Sunflower	Roasted sunflower seeds are dry enough to grind into a medium-grained flour that works in everything from cookies to nut balls.
Pumpkin	Like sunflower seeds, roasted pumpkin seeds are perfect for including in nut balls and other sweet-savory treats.

LEGUME FLOURS

Bean flours are high in protein and are great additions to savory crusts and breads. Because they don't have oily germs, bean flours can be stored in a cool, dark cupboard rather than the refrigerator.

LEGUME/FLOUR	TASTE & BEST USE
Black bean	The flour is perfect for hearty Southwestern flatbreads, and the whole cooked beans are great puréed into dips.
White bean	White bean flour is milder than black bean and makes for a calm backdrop in savory settings, especially crusts and flatbreads.
Chickpea (garbanzo)	Chickpea's distinctive flavor shines through in the flour, making it perfect to use for Mediterranean and Indian dishes and baked goods.
Fava bean	Favas are another not-too-strong bean that's commonly used as a blending element in savory flour blends.
Soybean	Whether you think it's beany or creamy, soybean flour is a very common element in gluten-free flour blends. However, because soy is a common allergen, I don't use soy flour in my recipes.
Yellow pea	These split peas are more mild than green peas—their flour provides a mild base for savory crusts, crepes, and flatbreads.
Green pea	Like the fresh peas, green pea flour is a pretty color, happily lending both its signature color and flavor to many savory baked goods.

ROOT/TUBER/STARCH FLOURS

Like short-grain rice, roots and tubers have a naturally high starch content that makes batters and doughs stick together. These flours also tend to have a lightening effect on the texture of baked goods. Because they contain virtually no fat, they can be stored in a cool, dark cupboard.

FOOD/FLOUR	TASTE & BEST USE
Sweet potato	Sweeter and less potato-y than potato flour, sweet potato flour is a tasty companion to corn flour when making savory flatbreads and griddle cakes.
Potato	The potato-iness of potato flour is somewhat surprising—griddle breads made with potato flour taste like potato chips!—making it a welcome addition to pizza crusts and other savory settings.
Plantain	This mild flour is perfect for pancakes, waffles, crepes, and anything else you'd like to be tender and pliable.
Tapioca (also called cassava, yuca, and/or manioc)	To me, this flour has a very powdery, dry, and metallic flavor, but tapioca can make breads more airy than most gluten-free flours can. Seeing as tapioca is not a nutritionally dense flour, though, I don't use it in my recipes.
Arrowroot	Arrowroot is very similar to tapioca in terms of uses, flavor, and lack of nutritional benefits. You won't find recipes with arrowroot starch in this book.

MISCELLANEOUS FLOURS

These flours don't really fit into any category—each one is unique in terms of flavor and behavior. That very refusal to fit in makes these my favorite flours! Like legumes and roots/tubers, you can store your miscellaneous flours in a cool, dark cupboard.

FOOD/FLOUR	TASTE & BEST USE
Coconut	Coconut flour absorbs amazing amounts of liquid, and its creamy, fiber-rich nature makes it a great flour to use in everything from cakes to quick breads. It's superb paired with chocolate!
Cocoa powder	This is an indispensable flour in brownies, chocolate cup-cakes, chocolate cake, chocolate smoothies, chocolate ice cream. . . anything you want to be rich and irresistible.
Carob powder	Not nearly as chocolaty as actual chocolate, carob powder still imparts a pleasantly creamy flavor to baked goods.
Mesquite	The dried and ground pods of the mesquite tree have an aromatic, caramel/molasses flavor that works well in cookies and spiced breads.

Make Your Own Reduced-Fat Milk (If You Must) and Save Money, Too

Do you insist on reduced-fat milk? If so, make your own by purchasing half the amount of milk you normally would—but buy whole milk!—and then add an equal amount of water to it. You've just spent half as much for a tastier, better-quality product, especially if you started out with milk from grass-fed cows. But really, your best option is to just drink whole milk. Why would you want a processed, non-whole milk?

DAIRY PRODUCTS

A general note about dairy products: Buy organic when you can, and if possible, buy dairy products that come from grass-fed animals. I won't get into the myriad details of why; that subject would and has taken up entire books. For now, let's just go with the common-sense approach that animals (and humans!) who eat what they have evolved to eat are going to be far healthier than those who don't. Cows are biologically equipped to eat grass—not soy or corn—and milk from healthy cows eating grass is nutritionally superior to milk from sick cows struggling to digest something their bodies aren't built to. Dairy products from grass-fed cows also taste better and are more fun to use because they can take on a starring role in your dishes.

But remember that while *organic* is an FDA-regulated term meaning that the cow is not being fed antibiotics, growth hormones, or genetically modified food, organic does not mean that an animal is grass-fed. Unfortunately, there is no standard for what "grass-fed" or "pastured" legally means—these labels are up to the producer and are self-regulated. Also bear in mind that small-scale local farmers may raise grass-fed livestock but may not have stamped-and-approved organic certification due to the costs and paperwork involved. The best way to find high-quality dairy products is to visit a farmers' market or two, talk to the farmers to see how they treat their animals, and talk to other shoppers to see what kind of experiences they've had with the producers and their products. You may even be able to visit the farm!

MILK

When it comes to milk, the whole-food principle still applies: Look for whole milk, which is the least processed variety, and grass-fed if possible, which is even more nutrient-dense.

Why whole? Whole milk contains about 3.5 percent milk fat, along with vitamins A and D. These vitamins are fat-soluble, meaning that they are best absorbed by the body when consumed with fat, making them a natural pair for full-fat milk (the milk fat helps our bodies access those vitamins in the milk). Another bonus point: Whole milk contains less lactose—that's the type of sugar found in dairy products—than reduced-fat milk does.

Recently, some whole milk producers have also begun offering unhomogenized milk, which is whole milk that has not been subjected to homogenization, the high-pressure (and often controversial) process that forcibly assimilates the cream (fat) into milk to prevent the two from naturally separating (and you from having to shake them back together). You can recognize nonhomogenized, or "creamline," milk by the cream cap at the top of the bottle. Should you be lucky enough to find unhomogenized whole milk, give it a try! Not only does it taste better, but you also get two products for the price of one, because you can pour off the cream and store it separately if you like. Or give the bottle a few shakes to disperse the cream and have whole milk. Another bonus of unhomogenized whole milk is that it's more likely to come from grass-fed cows.

CREAM

Aside from seeking out cream from grass-fed cows, another thing you might want to consider when choosing your cream is how it was pasteurized. While ultra high temperature (UHT) pasteurization makes a dairy product last longer, it is a controversial process that is said to change the chemical structure of the milk proteins and may interfere with digestion. Not only that, but whipping UHT cream can be a frustrating and lengthy process! Look for heavy whipping cream that isn't labeled UHT if at all possible.

Creams & Their Fat Percentages

Half-and-half:
10.5% to 18%

Light cream / Table cream:
18% to 30%

Medium cream:
25%

Whipping cream / Light cream:
30% to 36%

Heavy whipping cream / Heavy cream:
At least 36%

How much fat your cream has also makes a big difference if you're trying to whip it into whipped cream (see recipe on page 163). To have satisfyingly airy peaks, you need heavy cream, also called "heavy whipping cream," which contains at least 36 percent fat. Buyer beware, however! Despite what the label implies, "whipping cream" is only 30 percent fat—that's not enough fat content to make for nicely whipped cream. "Heavy cream" or "heavy whipping cream" is what you want.

If you're looking for cream to add to soup, sauces, or coffee, light cream or half-and-half works just as well as heavy cream. Again, try to find grass-fed products that aren't UHT.

PROBIOTIC DAIRY PRODUCTS

People of many cultures traditionally allow their milks and creams to ferment before consuming them or using them to make other products. Kumis, for example, is a fermented mare's milk that has been a staple of Central Asian cuisines for thousands of years. Kefir, which is fermented from either cow, sheep, or goat's milk, comes from the Caucasus region (the border area between Europe and Asia) and is now readily available in the United States. Smen is a fermented Moroccan butter prized for its pungent, full flavor. Like yogurt, all of these products are considered probiotic. Kefir in particular is becoming increasingly popular in the United States as more and more people realize that probiotic foods are essential to a healthy lifestyle.

But what does *probiotic* mean? Culturing, fermenting, and/or souring dairy products results in the rich growth of beneficial bacteria and enzymes—also known as probiotics. Regularly consuming probiotics makes our entire digestive system chug along better, improving our ability to digest whatever we eat. Seeing as all of our body systems depend upon nutrients we absorb from our food, what we eat (and don't eat) determines much of our overall health. Small wonder that so many traditional cuisines feature fermented foods!

BUTTER

Butter is churned cream (buttermilk is the liquid that falls away from the knob of butter during the churning process), and it can be made from either fresh cream or cultured cream. The latter has been fermented to give it the probiotic qualities mentioned above. Cultured butter has a richer, fuller flavor and is the traditional way butter is made in many European countries. Some Stateside creameries also make cultured butter.

Both types of butter come in two varieties: salted and unsalted (also called sweet). According to *The Joy of Cooking*, there's about 3/8 teaspoon of salt in a stick of salted butter. Doesn't sound like much, but it can add up. Cookie recipes, for example, often call for two sticks of butter. That's 3/4 teaspoon of salt. Not an insignificant amount! Whether you choose salted or unsalted is up to you—just be sure to account for the salt when baking. All recipes in this book use salted butter. You can use either fresh or cultured butter, whichever your taste buds prefer.

BUTTERMILK

As mentioned above, traditional buttermilk is the tangy liquid left over after butter churning. The reason buttermilk is so sour is that as it sits around and is allowed to ferment, bacteria gobble up the milk sugar, or lactose. The longer the bacteria gobbles, the more sour the buttermilk—or any fermented product—will taste. (Less sugar = more tartness.) American Southern cooks are particularly keen on buttermilk because the warm Southern climate lends itself to speedy buttermilk fermentation. That's why traditional Southern recipes are more likely to feature buttermilk than fresh milk.

Commercial buttermilks today, however, are artificially cultured by adding lactic acid bacteria to pasteurized milk. If you happen to get your hands on the real deal, you'll notice that it's thinner than commercial buttermilk, plus it'll have flecks of butter floating in it. If you don't have access to traditionally made buttermilk, try to find a whole-milk buttermilk. Reduced-fat buttermilk has less flavor and more additives in the form of stabilizers and thickeners.

SOUR CREAM AND CRÈME FRAÎCHE

Whereas sour cream used to be just that—"soured cream"—which was cultured naturally, many varieties today contain added fillers and ingredients. For best results, look for brands with a single ingredient: "cultured cream."

Sour cream imparts a deep richness to baked goods and makes a tasty garnish for many cooked dishes. Crème fraîche (or "fresh cream") is very similar to sour cream, albeit originating in Europe rather than the American South. Crème fraîche also tends to be produced on a much smaller scale and is often made with milk from grass-fed cows, making it richer and more flavorful than sour cream.

YOGURT

Yogurt can be a wonderful thing or a terrible thing. Wonderful yogurt is made from milk, cream, and probiotic cultures. Terrible yogurt contains far too many ingredients, most of which are sugars and artificial flavors. Most yogurts on American grocery store shelves fall into the latter category. Sad but true—just read a few of the ingredient lists on the yogurt containers the next time you're at the store and you'll see what I mean.

The best way to always have wonderful yogurt on hand is to buy plain, whole-milk yogurt and then sweeten/flavor it yourself. Honey, maple syrup, cut-up fresh fruit, and unsweetened cocoa powder are just a few ways to do that. Purchasing whole-milk plain yogurt also saves money, because you can make several small-batch flavors from one tub of yogurt instead of buying a dozen different varieties.

Greek yogurt is yogurt that has been double-strained. More of the whey—that's the liquid that rises to the top—drains out during that process, resulting in a thicker, creamier yogurt (and because the lactose is in the whey, Greek yogurt is also less sugary). I almost always use plain whole-milk Greek yogurt in place of sour cream because it has the same consistency but a fresher, more pleasing taste. You can also take it one step further by straining your Greek yogurt to make fresh cream cheese (see page 141).

CHEESE

Unlike fresh cheeses like cream cheese and cottage cheese, which are typically only a few days or weeks old and have a softer texture, aged cheeses ferment anywhere from a few months to a few years. These cheeses are hard in texture and have much stronger flavors than fresh-style cheeses. Aged cheeses also contain less lactose than fresh cheeses do, so if you're lactose-intolerant, you may have better luck with cheeses aged for a year or longer.

The variety of cheeses available continues to expand, with cheeses made from cow's, goat's, sheep's, and even buffalo's milk. When cheesemakers use milk and cream from grass-fed animals to make their cheeses, complex flavors result. Much like wine, cheese is referred to as having "terroir," or a sense of place that reflects everything from what the weather was like (more rain = lusher grass = more flavorful milk and cheese) to what kinds of plants the animals ate. That means that when you opt for cheese from grass-fed animals, each wedge or slice will be a new taste adventure!

EGGS

High-quality eggs are crucial to gluten-free baking success, because they provide much stronger structure along with improved nutrition and flavor. You'll recognize an egg from a free-range hen when you see one because the yolk will be a brilliant orange, difficult to pierce with a fork when scrambling, and easier to separate from the white because it stubbornly retains its shape. The white will be thicker and stronger, too, and the shell will be harder to break. In essence, a well-fed hen produces a sturdy, highly nutritious egg!

If you can, seek out eggs from pastured or free-range hens. Farmers' markets are a good place to find these eggs; cowshares and farmshares also provide opportunities to connect with local farmers who sell free-range eggs. Two of my favorites websites for finding such sources are www.localharvest.org and www.eatwild.com. Along with real-time information on where the farmers are, these sites also offer more information on the benefits of switching to grass-fed animal products.

OILS

Evaluating oil quality is easy when you think about the coleslaw scenario. Imagine it's a sweltering-hot bright summer day. Would you leave a container of coleslaw sitting on the sunny front seat of your car and then eat it several hours later? No—it's gone rancid. But would you take that same container of coleslaw and leave it tucked under the seat on a freezing-cold, overcast wintery night for a few hours and then eat it later? Sure. The coleslaw scenario is a great illustration of what makes fats/oils go bad: heat, light, and time. Pressure and chemicals play a role, too.

When you're looking at a refined oil, you're looking at an oil that's been subjected to all the factors that turn an oil rancid. That's why part of the refining process includes deodorizing and bleaching—nobody would buy a stinky, rancid oil. People do, however, think they're getting a good deal when the oil they buy "never goes bad." But think again about how that oil was processed before it reached the store shelf: exposure to extreme heat, light, pressure, and chemicals, followed by bleaching and deodorizing. While this all may make it possible to cook the oil at a high heat without it bursting into smoke or flames, these oils are far from natural.

Unrefined oils offer far more nutritional benefits and far better flavor than their highly refined and cheaply packaged counterparts do, so opt for unrefined oils whenever possible. Look for the following terms when purchasing, which mean that an oil has been gently treated and that its nutrients, flavor, and aroma are intact:

- Extra-virgin (this generally only applies to olive oil, although manufacturers of other oils are starting to use it as well)
- Unrefined

How to Tell Whether Your Egg Is Fresh

Want to know whether your eggs are still fresh? Place them in a bowl of cold water. If they sink to the bottom of the bowl, they're still fresh; if they float, toss them. Floating means that they've been sitting around long enough for enough air to leach into the shell and make an airbag at the top. That being said, if you're going to hard-boil an egg, it's better to hard-boil one that's at least three days old. A spanking-fresh egg is very difficult to peel after it's boiled.

If you don't see either of the above terms on the label or if you do see any of these terms listed below, the oil is refined:

- Virgin (you'll see this a lot on olive oil labels)
- Pomace (this is an industrial-grade olive oil that is made from processing the scraps of olives that are left over after the good-quality oil has been pressed from them)

For the sake of your health and for the sake of flavor, stick to unrefined oils when cooking and baking. And once you've chosen your oil, be sure to store it properly and use according to its advised upper limit for heat. (Many top-notch oil producers clearly state the maximum limit for each particular oil—look for a little picture of a thermometer and the accompanying temperature. Unrefined peanut oil, for example, generally has a limit of 395°F [202°C].) If the oil you're using doesn't state its upper limit for heat, glance at the nutrition label to see whether it is mostly composed of polyunsaturated, monounsaturated, or saturated fat. This ratio will help you determine how to use any given oil. To be more specific:

- Oils that are primarily saturated fat can be stored at room temperature and can be heated up to 400°F (204°C) and sometimes even 450°F (232°C). If you plan on storing them for more than a year, put them in the refrigerator to extend their life.
- Oils that are primarily monounsaturated fat can handle being heated up to 300°F (149°C) to 350°F (177°C). They can be stored in the refrigerator or in a cool and dark place; use these oils within six months if stored at room temperature or a year if stored in the refrigerator.
- Polyunsaturated oils should never be heated and should always be stored in the refrigerator. Use within six months.

Other than the crucial temperature component, choose your oil based on the type of flavor you prefer and what works best for the dish. Unrefined oils retain an incredible aroma and therefore loads of flavor. For example, you can make peanut cookies very peanutty just by using unrefined peanut oil! Extra-virgin olive oil imparts a fruity undernote to baked goods; unrefined sesame oil provides a buttery, nutty backdrop. Even the not-to-be-heated polyunsaturated oils like walnut and pecan can be incorporated into your baked goods—just drizzle a hint over whatever you're serving right before you serve it (walnut oil on pancakes . . . mmm).

SWEETENERS
While it's a bad idea to make any kind of sweetener the mainstay of your diet, there's a big difference between natural sweeteners and refined sugars: the former contain some nutritious elements along with sweetness, but the latter do not. And natural sweeteners contribute flavor, too. From a health standpoint as well as a culinary one, you're better off swapping refined sugars for natural sweeteners. Let's break natural sweeteners down into categories to make them easier to explore.

LIQUID SWEETENERS
Looking for something sweet to drizzle or stir into a beverage? Luckily, you'll find plenty of natural, unrefined options.

Maple Syrup

Maple is by far my favorite sweetener: It pairs wonderfully with chocolate, spices, nuts, coconut, you name it. Americans and Canadians are lucky, because our countries are the only ones that produce maple syrup in any quantity.

When looking at maple syrup, make sure it really is maple syrup—cheap brands like Aunt Jemima and Log Cabin are corn syrup and chemicals, not maple syrup. And remember that Grade B is more flavorful and has a richer color than Grade A. Some also say it has slightly more nutrients, but the jury is still out on that point. Either one is a great choice.

Honey

Honey is one of my top choices for sweeteners, especially if it's local and raw (raw honey contains live enzymes). Because honey attracts moisture from the air, it helps keep baked goods soft and moist, and because it's so sweet, a little goes a long way. Different strains of honey even have markedly different flavors stemming from the particular flowers the bees frequent.

Molasses

Like refined cane sugar, molasses is made from sugarcane—but that's where the similarity stops. Whereas refined sugars have been stripped of their nutrients, molasses is loaded with them. Blackstrap molasses is the most nutrient-rich type, with high levels of potassium, iron, calcium, and magnesium. It has an earthy/bitter aspect to its sweetness and works best when paired with strong spices like ginger and cinnamon.

Sorghum Syrup

Don't let high-fructose corn syrup ruin your impression of all grain-based syrups—sorghum syrup has been a favored sweetener in the United States since the 1850s. It can be tricky to find, but if you do find it (it's also called sorghum molasses), you can use it in the same way you'd use maple syrup, although its flavor hovers a little closer to molasses.

Brown Rice Syrup

This medium-brown liquid sweetener has a smooth, slightly caramelized sweetness that pairs well with not too strongly flavored baked goods. The only drawback is that you need to use a fair amount of it for your baked items to be moderately sweet.

Date Syrup and Coconut Nectar

We don't see these syrups much in the United States, but they're

---

Looking for the Real Deal

Aunt Jemima's Original Syrup ingredients: Corn syrup, high-fructose corn syrup, water, cellulose gum, caramel color, salt, sodium benzoate and sorbic acid (preservatives), artificial and natural flavors, sodium hexametaphosphate

100% Pure Maple Syrup ingredients: Maple syrup

popular in tropical regions. Date syrup comes from date palm trees; coconut nectar comes from coconut palms. Date syrup is dark-colored and offers a robust date flavor along with its sweetness. Coconut nectar tastes a little sweeter (and its flavor is more neutral), yet is surprisingly low on the glycemic index, which is to say that it won't cause as much of a spike in blood sugar levels as many other sweeteners do.

Tapioca Syrup

What we call "tapioca," others call "cassava" (in Africa), "manioc" (in Southeast Asia), and "yuca" (in Central and South America). No matter its name, it's a long tuber that can be boiled and eaten in chunks; boiled and pounded into a fluffy mash; rolled into pearls and cooked; dried and powdered to use as a starch; or boiled down to be made into a syrup. As a syrup, it tastes mildly sweet and rather malty. But be warned: It takes a lot of tapioca syrup to make anything taste sweet, so you might want to use it for drizzling rather than baking.

Yacón Syrup

This is another tropical tuber that can be made into a syrup, albeit a darker and stronger-tasting one than tapioca syrup. It's grown primarily in the Andes region of South America and is becoming more and more popular in the United States. Its flavor most closely matches that of blackstrap molasses.

SOLID SWEETENERS

Avoiding refined white sugar is easy when you have these natural options to choose from. Try these out to find your favorites!

Rapadura, Jaggery, or Panela

These sugars (a.k.a. "cone sugars") are all made by crushing sugarcane to extract its juice, boiling the juice to thicken it, and then finally pouring the thickened syrup into molds to dry. Once the sugar syrup dries, it's tapped out of the molds and sold in its distinctive cone shape. To use a cone sugar, cut off a chunk of it, and then chop or grind it until you've reached the desired texture. (In Costa Rica, locals pour hot water over a small chunk of rapadura, stir until smooth, and enjoy their "agua dulce"—which has a faint caramel flavor—with breakfast.) Jaggery, a popular sweetener in India, is sometimes also made from date palm sap.

Sucanat (Sugar Cane Natural)

This is the queen of unrefined sugars. It's very similar to the cone sugars in the sense that it's relatively nutrient-dense, unrefined

Upgrading Powdered Sugar

Want to avoid refined powdered sugar? Powder sucanat in a coffee/spice grinder! Grind for a few seconds and you'll have a fragrant, flavorful powdered sugar to use in chiffon cakes, frosting, or sweetened beverages like hot chocolate.

Dairy Tips for Those Who Are Lactose-Intolerant or Sensitive to Cow's Milk

If you have dairy difficulties, here are several suggestions that might help. Not all dairy products are created equal, and with a little know-how, you may find there are quite a few you can enjoy with no ill side effects.

- Raw milk is typically easier to digest than pasteurized milk because lactase—the enzyme responsible for breaking down lactose—is present in raw milk, whereas it is no longer present in pasteurized milk because it's been destroyed by heat. Interestingly, the majority of the world's adults don't produce the lactase needed to digest lactose. For those who don't, the lactase naturally present in raw milk often does the trick. Raw milk regulations vary by state, so while raw milk can be sold off the shelf in some states (such as California), it must be purchased directly from the farmer as part of a cowshare in others (that's how I get mine in Michigan). Raw-milk cheeses, on the other hand, are now available in nearly every grocery store across the country. If you find that you can easily digest raw-milk cheese and want to find out more about getting raw milk where you live, check out www.realmilk.com or do an online search.

- You can always substitute coconut milk for dairy milk. In fact, even if you're perfectly fine with dairy products, try using coconut milk anyway! It's fantastic in smoothies, ice cream, baked goods, and especially in savory curries and sauces (like the Indonesian Curried Peanut Pasta on page 96).

- Some individuals are sensitive to cow's milk but not to goat or sheep's milk. Goat's milk is now sold in most stores, and goat- and sheep-milk cheeses are readily available.

- Fermented dairy products contain little if any lactose, because as the bacterial cultures grow (i.e., fermentation occurs), they consume the lactose and transform it into lactic acid. Many lactose-intolerant individuals can handle small amounts of yogurt, kefir, sour cream, cultured butter, buttermilk, or anything that's fermented/cultured.

- Ghee is clarified butter—that is, butter that's been heated to evaporate its moisture. Nearly all of its milk solids are strained off in the process, too, so it's usually lactose- and casein-free. Ghee can also handle higher temperatures than butter can, making ghee ideal for high-heat applications. Many stores now sell ghee in the dairy case.

- Aged cheeses contain less lactose than fresh cheeses do, and therefore may be better tolerated.

cane juice with a mild caramel flavor. Just opening a bag of sucanat for the first time is an experi-ence—that's what sugarcane is supposed to smell (and taste) like! Unlike cone sugars, sucanat comes granulated and can therefore be measured out easily. Substitute it 1:1 for refined white sugar.

Date Sugar

Date sugar is made by grinding dried dates. The resulting "sugar" is moist and chewy, and tastes like dates, albeit not as sweet. This sweetener is too coarse to use in finely textured baked goods, but it works wonderfully as a topping or in streusel.

Maple Sugar

Maple sugar is made by letting maple syrup dry out and harden into flakes. It retains a fragrant maple flavor and can be used as a 1:1 substitute for refined white sugar. It can be expensive, though, so you may want to use it as a finishing sprinkle/garnish.

SECTION HIGHLIGHTS

- Whole grains and flours are important elements of healthier cooking and baking; so are good-quality eggs and dairy products. Having so many options makes cooking and baking a lot more fun (and deliciously nutritious)!

- Unrefined oils have more flavor, nutrition, and culinary potential than refined oils do.

- Not only are natural sweeteners readily available, but they also offer more flavor and nutrition than refined sweeteners do. Time to explore some new possibilities!

Chapter 5 | Core Concepts of Gluten-Free Baking

READY, SET, BAKE!

You know what "the good stuff" is now, so let's put those tasty ingredients to good use! In this chapter, you'll find tips and techniques for gluten-free baking success, plus a quick rundown of ways to tweak your favorite baked goods to make them gluten-free (and more nutritious). You'll also see how easy it is to make your own flour . . . and how much easier it is to bake and cook in a gluten-free kitchen. No more sticky messes!

ESSENTIAL INGREDIENTS

We've already talked about how important it is to use quality ingredients, so now let's talk about practical ways to make the most out of those ingredients, including cost-saving tips for making your own flour. You'll also learn about the building blocks of baking so that you'll be better-equipped to translate your favorite recipes into new gluten-free classics.

FLOUR

Grinding your own flour is the best way to have fresh, nutritious, protein-rich flour.

When It Comes to DIY Flours:

- Designate a coffee/spice grinder (or food processor) for flour-grinding duty. These grinders cost less than twenty dollars and are immensely useful in a gluten-free kitchen.
- In about ten seconds, you can make flour from pumpkin seeds, chia seeds, flaxseeds, poppy seeds, sunflower seeds, rolled oats, quinoa, teff, sliced almonds, toasted pine nuts, toasted pecans, toasted walnuts, and toasted sesame seeds. Just grind in pulses until a fine consistency is reached; use a sifter to remove larger bits if there are any.
- If you have a high-powered blender/grinder like a Vitamix, you can grind anything into flour, even hard grains like brown rice and buckwheat or hard nuts like whole hazelnuts.
- If you buy an ingredient in its whole form, then you have two options: grind it or use it whole. Convenient and thrifty! Also, some ingredients are readily available and inexpensive in their whole forms, but not as flour.

When It Comes to Store-Bought Flours:

- Choose whole-food flours rather than their refined versions. (Potato flour instead of potato starch, corn flour instead of cornstarch, brown rice flour instead of white rice flour, etc.)
- Store grain, seed, and nut flours and meals in the refrigerator at all times to prolong their life. This includes cornmeal!
- Make sure bags of flour are securely resealed after you've opened them. Better yet, store your opened flours in tightly closed glass containers.
- Buy flour from stores with high turnover rates. Produce-focused stores, health-food/natural-food stores, and online specialty stores like Bob's Red Mill are your best bets for finding a good variety of fresh flours.
- Be open-minded, have fun, and experiment! Check out "Gluten-Free Flour Families" (page 21) to see what various flours have in common and how you might want to use them.

Quick & Easy Gluten-Free Transformations

You'll find specific recipes for most of these items throughout this book, but here's a quick glance at some classic dishes that can go from off-limits to gluten-free with a slight tweak.

FOOD	GLUTEN-FREE TWEAK
Roux-based sauces	Use a mild and medium-starch flour such as brown rice or corn flour in place of wheat.
Grain salads	Use gluten-free grains such as millet, quinoa, or rice rather than bulgur or couscous.
Pasta dishes	Choose from a variety of gluten-free pastas on the market, including rice-, quinoa-, and corn-based pastas.
Crepes	Nearly any fine-milled flour works for crepes—all you have to decide is whether you'd prefer savory or sweet!
Pies, cobblers, slumps, buckles, and grunts	These fruit-based desserts are traditionally meant to be tender and are made with plenty of butter, which means that they're ideal for making with gluten-free flours.
Cookies	Again, cookies are made rich with lots of butter and/or nuts, which means you don't need gluten to make a great cookie—most gluten-free flours are ideally suited for cookies.
Quick breads	Quick breads are meant to be tender and moist, so nut flours are especially wonderful here.
Cornbread	From smooth, rich spoonbreads to firm cornbread sweetened with apples, these traditional treats are usually made with corn, not wheat.
Shortbread	These buttery treats do just fine with mild-tasting flours such as brown rice or corn—or make a statement with teff or amaranth.
Muffins and cupcakes	The stars of gluten-free baking, muffins and cupcakes offer endless options—they're the culinary equivalent of having a palette of ingredients in your hand.
Cakes	Cakes are also prime candidates for making gluten-free, because the goal of a cake is to be tender and delicate rather than hearty and chewy.
Bar cookies	Like cakes and muffins, you have nearly all the gluten-free flours at your disposal when it comes to making bar cookies (brownies, lemon squares, etc.).
Frozen desserts	Ice cream, frozen yogurt, and gelato are usually naturally gluten-free, unless they contain cookie dough or other additions.
Rice and corn puddings	Puddings have been a staple since colonial times, and traditional rice and corn puddings have never contained gluten.
Egg-based dishes	When eggs play a starring role, gluten is secondary if not absent, so using brown rice flour rather than wheat flour in your custard, mousse, or soufflé won't bother it a bit.
Fruit-based desserts	Sautéed fruit, stuffed and baked fruit, fruit that's been simmered into a fragrant compote . . . none of these need any gluten.
Biscotti	Seeing as the goal here is to be crunchy and crumbly, these airy Italian cookies are perfectly suited to being made gluten-free.

Food	Gluten-Free Tweak
Nut balls	Protein-rich and satisfying nut balls are a toothsome combination of nuts, seeds, and dried fruit and contain no gluten.
Truffles	Rich and decadent chocolates are rarely made with gluten.
Cheesecakes	The only gluten here is in the crust, so swapping out wheat for gluten-free flours is a snap.
Waffles	Whether you're talking Belgian or standard waffles, gluten-free flours can easily be swapped in, and as long as you do a good job of greasing your waffle iron, no gluten = no worries.
Samosas	Samosas, empanadas, pasties, and other stuffed bread "packages" can be made using gluten-free flours and a bit of judicious rolling and patting using plastic wrap.
Dumplings	Use starchier flours such as potato, sticky rice, and plantain to create soft and sticky dough for dumplings.
Bread crumbs/ breading	Many things can be bread crumbs: almond flour, grated Parmesan, crushed tortilla or vegetable chips, cornmeal, crushed puffed rice, and so on.
Soy sauce	Soy sauce is usually brewed with wheat, but tamari usually is not—check the labels to be sure.
Pilafs	These rice-based dishes are featured in every world cuisine and are almost always gluten-free.
Cereals/ granola	Gluten-free cereal and granola options abound, and besides, it's easy to make your own cereals/granolas exactly the way you want them.
Pancakes	From coconut to corn flour, gluten-free flours will lend your pancakes a unique flavor and texture.
Pizzas	Savory gluten-free swaps and combinations such as corn, brown rice, chickpea, and potato flours make wonderfully flavorful crusts.
Beer	More and more gluten-free beers are hitting the market; most are made with rice, millet, corn, and/or sorghum.
Bread used to thicken soups and sauces	Grains and starchy vegetables such as potatoes make great thickeners, or you can use leftover gluten-free bread to make your gazpacho thicker.
Breads	Flatbreads such as tortillas, johnnycakes, and rice fritters are already gluten-free.
Biscuits and scones	Depending on what you'd like to pair them with, these savory, butter-rich breads can be made with anything from pea flour to quinoa flour.
Stuffing	Chestnut stuffing, wild rice stuffing, and cornbread stuffing have always been welcome at the table, and they're almost always gluten-free.
Crusts	Crusts for casseroles, potpies, quiches, and tarts can just as easily be made with decidedly savory flours such as fava bean, chickpea, and sweet potato, or with sweeter flours such as sorghum and mesquite.
Crackers and chips	Corn chips, brown rice crackers, root chips, even chickpea chips are readily available on store shelves, or make your own by roasting thinly sliced veggies.

Advantages of Using Gluten-Free Flours

While that pesky gluten offers some handy benefits when it comes to baking and cooking, gluten-free baking has advantages, too. Here are a few reasons why a gluten-free foodstyle makes life in the kitchen a lot more fun!

- Once you stop using wheat as your only flour, you'll get to experience a wealth of different flours, each with its own unique taste, texture, and suitability.
- Taking advantage of a variety of gluten-free flours means you'll have access to far more nutrients than you'd get from just wheat.
- From a culinary standpoint, welcoming different flours into your kitchen will allow you to choose your flours based on how their flavor will complement your final dish. The recipes in this book will give you plenty of inspiration and guidance as you get creative with your flours.
- Gluten-free baking is often easier than gluten-based baking. Free-form biscuits can be made by dropping spoonfuls of dough onto a baking sheet. Pizza dough can be patted into place. No rolling or stretching needed!
- Many quick bread recipes (think banana and pumpkin bread) warn you not to overstir wheat-based batters. That's because stirring can overwork the gluten and make the final product tough. With gluten-free flours, you no longer have to worry about accidentally overstirring and ruining the texture of your bread.
- Along with quick breads, plenty of other baked goods are meant to be tender-crumbed: cupcakes, pancakes, cakes, muffins, biscuits, shortbreads, many types of cookies, crepes, waffles, pies, cobblers, and so on. Using gluten-free flours guarantees that you'll have tender-crumbed results.
- Part of gluten's charm is that it's very sticky and holds things together. That same stickiness, however, often makes bowls and utensils difficult to clean. You're going to love how much more quickly you can clean up your kitchen after using gluten-free flours.

As with any new project or idea, the trick to embracing a gluten-free foodstyle is to have an open mind and be willing to try new things. Life's a tasty adventure!

FATS AND LIQUIDS

Fats are essential for creating moisture and richness, carrying flavors, and providing a luxurious mouthfeel. Biscotti, for example, while delicious in its crunchy fashion, could not be described as "moist and rich." Nor could an angel cake, nor a baked meringue. That's because those items contain very little fat.

Many fats—milk, oils, melted butter, cream—are also liquids and contribute to the consistency of both the batter and the final product. In general, "batter" is a thickly pourable mixture (i.e., it contains more liquid), while "dough" is usually stiff enough to be rolled out, pressed into place, or otherwise shaped. Baked goods and stove-cooked breads vary greatly in how much liquid—and fat—they contain.

Whole milk plays many valuable roles in baked goods. The milk sugar (lactose) milk contains browns nicely when baked, the proteins milk contains help form the structure of whatever you're baking, and even though whole milk is only about 4 percent fat, it still provides a backdrop of richness and flavor.

When baking with whole grains, you'll usually need extra liquid/fat to prevent the final baked good from becoming too dry. That means the raw batter/dough should look wetter than what you've seen with wheat-based baking (in other words, non-whole-grain baking). If the final product is still too dry, moisten it by pouring on a little milk or cream before serving. An extra pat of butter or drizzle of unrefined oil is always nice, too!

LEAVENERS

When it comes to baked goods, leavening is the element that'll make or break you. Cakes and breads and muffins all rise or fall because of the presence or lack of leavening. (Flatbreads, on the other hand, are blessedly free of leavening considerations because . . . well . . . they're flat.)

Baking soda and baking powder are common chemical leaveners that release tiny carbon dioxide gas bubbles when mixed with a liquid. Though they work in a similar fashion, they are not interchangeable. Baking soda needs to be combined with an acid and a liquid in order to react and create the gas bubbles; baking powder is a premixed combination of baking soda and an acid, so all it needs to launch itself into action is the liquid. For example, recipes that include a strong acidic ingredient such as yogurt, sour cream, or molasses generally call for baking soda. Recipes that do not include sufficiently acidic ingredients call for baking powder instead.

The most crucial point to remember is that baking soda (when used with an acid) is four times stronger than baking powder. So if you mistakenly use 1 teaspoon of baking soda rather than the 1 teaspoon of baking powder that's called for, you've inadvertently quadrupled your leavening. This will leave you with a concave muffin or cake, because if you overleaven something, all the bubbles created in the batter will run together, form one giant bubble, pop, and cause the batter to collapse in on itself. (But the good news is that you can save your overleavened baked goods by repurposing them into a new creation. The first time I made the Blueberry-Buckwheat Yogurt Muffins [page 45], I overleavened them and wound up with seriously indented muffins. The solution? I pulled them out of their cups, piled the oversized moist crumbs onto a large plate, and called it Jumblecake. People love getting to sample new culinary creations!)

Aside from common chemical leaveners such as baking soda and baking powder, bakers can also employ physical leaveners, which are techniques, not ingredients, such as creaming butter until it's soft and fluffy, whipping cream until it forms medium-stiff mounds, gently folding batter, and beating egg whites until they're peaked. All of these techniques help lighten the texture of baked goods.

PROTEINS

Because gluten is a protein, going without it means your baked goods will work best if you make up for that lost protein. Not to worry—you can easily do so by using high-protein flours such as nut flours, seed flours, and bean flours, plus there's plenty of protein in eggs and dairy products. With your whole-grain flours and whole-food ingredients, you won't be lacking for protein.

Avoiding Starches

Most commercially available gluten-free baked goods are based on starch—cornstarch, potato starch, and tapioca starch—in an attempt to imitate non-whole-grain breads. But because this book focuses on wholesome gluten-free dishes, nutrient-void starches are not going to get any play. Instead, we'll be using whole-food versions of naturally starchy flours, such as potato flour (not potato starch) and corn flour (not cornstarch).

Avoiding Gums

Vegetable gums are sometimes used to thicken and bind gluten-free baked goods. You might come across guar gum, xanthan gum, perhaps even locust bean gum in your grocery store. These gums provide a thickening/binding effect, but they're also slippery and difficult to clean off of hands, bowls, and utensils. I don't use gums in my recipes.

SWEETENERS

While the standard sweetener has become refined white sugar, many kinds of natural sweeteners can be used in gluten-free baking, and with delicious results (see the "Sweeteners" section on page 30). Natural sweeteners provide a sweet taste as well as specific textures and flavors. The way they caramelize when heated—which creates a deepened flavor as well as a browning effect—and how they behave in the baking makes a big difference as to how your baked item tastes.

Sugars also preserve foods, which is another reason why our foods have become more and more sugared over the years. Fruitcake is a classic case of preserving by sugaring. But while sugar preserves foods, it also expands our waistlines and leads to chronic diseases such as diabetes, obesity, heart disease, and inflammatory conditions. Refined sugar also impairs our immune systems and makes us more susceptible to opportunistic viruses, bacteria, and cancer. That's why you won't find any recipes with white sugar in this book.

Instead, the recipes you'll find here feature natural, less-refined sweeteners that retain more of their nutritional content. We'll also be using a lot less overall sweetener than traditional recipes use. A nice side effect of using natural sweeteners (and less of them) is that you'll taste more flavor. It doesn't take long to swap your sweet tooth for happier taste buds and improved health!

ESSENTIAL TECHNIQUES

Tip #1: Handle the Dough as Little as Possible When Shaping It

Rather than sticking to itself, gluten-free dough tends to stick to what's touching it—your hands, a rolling pin, the countertop, etc. But if you employ these simple handling techniques, dealing with it is a snap:

- Instead of rolling out dough and cutting it into shapes, make free-form biscuits, scones, cookies, and so on by spooning rough mounds of dough onto parchment-covered baking sheets.
- Press and pat your crusts into their pans instead of rolling them out.
- When you do roll out dough, place a sheet of plastic wrap on top of and underneath the dough so that it can't stick to the rolling pin or the countertop.
- For dough-wrapped packages such as empanandas, calzones, and samosas, brush the finished packages with oil or melted butter and bake them instead of frying them.
- When dealing with dough, make sure you have extra flour in a nearby bowl for flouring your hands so that the dough is less likely to stick to you.

Tip #2: Make the Most of Your Leaveners

Leavening is crucial to the success of all baked goods, especially gluten-free baked goods! Be sure to:

- Take advantage of leavening techniques. Cream your butter well, beat your eggs thoroughly, and fold batters when indicated. The end results are worth a few extra minutes of prep.
- Be prepared before adding your ingredient leaveners. Make sure the oven is preheated, pans are greased, and whatever tools you'll need—whisk, spatula, wooden spoon—are on hand.
- Move quickly once you've combined the baking powder/soda with any wet ingredients. This is even more important for aluminum-free baking powder because the leavening reaction kicks in almost immediately. If you delay, you'll likely be left with a rose-too-soon-and-then-fell baked item.

SECTION HIGHLIGHTS

Understanding essential ingredients and techniques makes gluten-free baking a lot less mysterious, plus you'll be better equipped to translate your favorite wheat-based recipes into gluten-free versions.

Many dishes and baked goods are gluten-free already or just require a slight (and tasty) tweak to make them gluten-free.

Notes: Suggested Recipe Ingredients

Animal Products

These are best sourced from grass-fed/pastured/free-range animals. These products are higher in nutritional quality and also taste and work better in recipes. Free-range eggs, for example, provide much better structure for baked goods than conventional eggs—and the animals providing these products have led healthier, more humane lives. Look for grass-fed/pastured/free-range versions of:

- Dairy products: cheese, milk, yogurt, butter, buttermilk, crème fraîche, etc.
- Meats: chicken, lamb, pork, beef, sausage, bacon, etc.
- Broth: chicken, beef
- Eggs

Produce

Avoid some of the top-sprayed fruits and vegetables (also known as the "Dirty Dozen"). Choosing organic versions of those top-sprayed items often means that the produce tastes better and has a more pleasing texture. I always opt for organic versions of the following:

- Apples (fresh, dried, applesauce)
- Greens (romaine, spinach, baby spinach, salad greens)
- Strawberries (fresh, frozen, jam)
- Corn (fresh, frozen, popcorn, corn tortillas)
- When I use the zest, citrus fruits (lemons, oranges, limes)
- Grapes

Seafood and Fish

Wild, sustainable seafood and fish offer better nutrition and flavor than farmed fish do (although some sustainable farming operations produce top-notch seafood and fish). For up-to-date information on this topic, including printable shopping guides for seafood and fish in your area, check out www.seafoodwatch.org. In the meantime, when shopping for seafood and fish, look for:

- Shrimp: wild-caught U.S. shrimp
- Salmon: wild salmon, particularly from Alaska
- Fish in general: whatever is wild-caught/sustainably farmed, seasonal, and plentiful in your area

Canned Goods

Most authorities now agree that BPA, a chemical used to line the interior of cans for canned products, could be problematic for our health (see more information on page 59). Fortunately, many companies now produce BPA-free canned goods. Look for BPA-free versions of canned:

- Beans: chickpeas, black beans, navy beans, Great Northern beans
- Seafood/fish: tuna, crab

Baking Ingredients

A few specific baking ingredients are worth seeking out for improved flavor and/or health reasons.

- Unsweetened cocoa powder: "natural" or "non-alkalized" (see more information on page 170)
- Baking powder: aluminum-free
- Corn products: organic corn flour, cornmeal, and polenta

PART III

HEALTHIER GLUTEN-FREE RECIPES

....

A Quick Guide to Recipe Codes
For those who have special dietary needs in addition to being gluten-free, you'll find these handy markers on all applicable recipes:

Nut-Free: These dishes do not include nut or coconut in any form.

Dairy-Free: These dishes do not contain milk, yogurt, cheese, butter, or any type of dairy.

Soy-Free: These dishes do not contain gluten-free tamari, edamame, or any type of soy product.

Egg-Free: These dishes do not contain eggs.

Vegetarian: These dishes do not contain meat, meat broth, seafood, or fish (they may contain dairy and eggs).

20 minutes or less: These dishes can be prepared in 20 minutes or less.

*See page 41 for ingredient notes: This refers back to some important information about ingredient sourcing and recommendations.

Chapter 6 | Breakfast Time: Waking Up with a Smile

Your day will be off to a great start with these satisfying, make-ahead breakfasts. (And yes, they're whole-grain, too!) No need to skip the most important meal of the day when it's so easy to enjoy a homemade morning meal. DIY cereal? Got it. Belgian waffles? Check. Waking up just got a lot more delicious.

■ DIY WHOLE-GRAIN CEREAL
Nut-Free (use non-nut milk), Dairy-Free (use nondairy milk), Soy-Free, Egg-Free, Vegetarian, 20 minutes or less

Making your own cereal tastes better and is better for you, plus homemade cereal costs a lot less than the standard non-whole-grain, oversugared version that comes in a fancy box. Use any gluten-free grain you like (leftovers are perfect for this!), such as: brown/black/purple/red/wild rice, quinoa, millet, gluten-free oats, amaranth, teff, buckwheat, or a combination!

Cooked grain of choice (see above)
Milk of choice (whole dairy milk*, nut milk, grain milk, or coconut milk)
See Notes on page 41

Toppings of choice (maple syrup, honey, date sugar, dried fruit, chopped or slivered nuts, fresh fruit, sprinkling of cinnamon or ginger, cocoa nibs, or unsweetened flaked, toasted coconut, etc.)

Combine all the ingredients the same way you'd combine a standard bowl of cereal: Scoop the whole grains into a bowl, then pour on the milk and add toppings. So easy! And because cooked grains keep for up to 1 week in the fridge, you can make one big batch on the weekend and have instant breakfasts all week long.

Yield: 1 serving

■ YOGURT YOUR WAY
Nut-Free, Soy-Free, Egg-Free, Vegetarian, 20 minutes or less

Start with plain whole-milk Greek yogurt, then let your imagination run wild! Feel free to experiment with various fruits, sweeteners, and spices. Or stir in chopped nuts, alternative extracts, or chunks of dark chocolate.

For Chocolate Yogurt:
2 tablespoons (10 g) unsweetened cocoa powder*
1 tablespoon (15 ml) maple syrup
½ cup (115 g) whole-milk plain Greek yogurt*

For Vanilla-Cinnamon Yogurt:
1 tablespoon (15 ml) maple syrup
½ teaspoon vanilla extract
½ teaspoon cinnamon
½ cup (115 g) whole-milk plain Greek yogurt*
See Notes on page 41

To make either version: Stir together with a small whisk or fork. Add more maple to taste if you like. Serve promptly or refrigerate for up to 3 days.

Yield: about ⅔ cup (154 g) each

◀ BLUEBERRY-BUCKWHEAT YOGURT MUFFINS

Soy-Free, Vegetarian

Blueberries naturally sweeten these muffins—all they need is a hint of sucanat. If you'd like your muffins to be sweeter, you can double up on the sucanat when you're making the batter.

1 cup (90 g) almond flour
1 cup (120 g) buckwheat flour
¼ cup (40 g) brown rice flour
¼ cup (40 g) sucanat
2 teaspoons (9 g) baking powder*
½ teaspoon baking soda
Dash of sea salt
1 teaspoon cinnamon

½ teaspoon nutmeg
¼ cup (60 ml) extra-virgin olive oil
2 eggs*
2 cups (345 g) whole-milk plain Greek yogurt*
1 teaspoon vanilla extract
6 ounces (170 g) fresh blueberries
See Notes on page 41

Preheat oven to 375°F (190°C, or gas mark 5) and line a muffin tin with 12 parchment-paper muffin cups.

In a large bowl, whisk together the flours, sucanat, baking powder, baking soda, salt, and spices. In another bowl, whisk together the oil, eggs, yogurt, and vanilla. Stir in the blueberries. Stir the wet ingredients into the dry ones until well blended.

Scoop the batter into muffin cups and bake for 25 minutes, or until a toothpick inserted into the center-most muffin comes out clean and warm. Leftover muffins can be refrigerated for up to 4 days.

Yield: 12 muffins

■ RICOTTA-INFUSED OAT & POPPY SEED MUFFINS

Nut-Free, Soy-Free, Vegetarian

Whole-milk ricotta cheese is incredibly creamy and fresh. If you can't find whole-milk ricotta, you can use whole-milk cottage cheese instead, preferably the small-curd variety.

¾ cup (90 g) millet or sorghum flour
1 cup (160 g) brown rice flour
½ cup (40 g) gluten-free rolled oats
1 tablespoon (14 g) baking powder*
½ teaspoon sea salt
¼ cup (35 g) poppy seeds
1 cup (250 g) fresh whole-milk ricotta cheese*

4 eggs*
¼ cup (85 g) honey
½ cup (120 ml) extra-virgin olive oil
1 cup (235 ml) whole milk*
2 teaspoons (10 ml) vanilla extract
See Notes on page 41

Preheat the oven to 375°F (190°C, or gas mark 5) and line 2 muffin tins with 18 parchment-paper muffin cups.

In a large bowl, whisk together the flours, oats, baking powder, salt, and seeds. In a medium bowl, whisk together the ricotta, eggs, honey, oil, milk, and vanilla. Pour the liquid ingredients into the dry ones and whisk well to combine.

Spoon the batter into the lined tins and bake for 20 to 22 minutes, or until a toothpick inserted into the center-most muffin comes out clean and warm.

Top baked muffins with additional ricotta and honey if you'd like. Leftover muffins can be refrigerated for up to 5 days.

Yield: 18 muffins

➤ Shred 1 small zucchini on
a box grater, then wring the
water out of the shredded
zucchini in small handfuls,
lightly packing the wrung-out
zucchini into a 1-cup measure
until you have 1 full cup.

■ ZUCCHINI, APPLE & PECAN QUICK BREAD WITH TEFF FLOUR

Soy-Free, Vegetarian

Teff is the world's smallest grain. It's also one of the staple grains of Africa—traditional Ethiopian bread, called injera, is made by mixing ground teff with water and letting it naturally ferment before making it into crepe-like flatbreads. You can grind teff into flour yourself if you have a high-speed blender or flour mill.

Butter or extra-virgin olive oil,
   for greasing pan
1 cup (90 g) almond flour
¾ cup (90 g) millet or sorghum flour
1 cup (200 g) teff flour
¾ cup (83 g) chopped pecans
1 teaspoon cinnamon
1 teaspoon allspice
1 teaspoon coriander
1 tablespoon (14 g) baking powder*
Dash of sea salt

1 cup (80 g) shredded and wrung-
   out zucchini (See Recipe Note)
¾ cup (175 g) whole milk*
2 eggs*
¼ cup (60 ml) maple syrup
1 large apple, core removed,
   finely chopped*
   (about 1 ½ cups, or 225 g)
1 teaspoon vanilla extract
½ cup (120 ml) extra-virgin olive
   oil, plus more for greasing pan
See Notes on page 41

Preheat the oven to 350°F (180°C, or gas mark 4). Grease a 9 x 5-inch (23 x 13 cm) glass loaf pan with butter.

In a large bowl, whisk together the flours, pecans, spices, baking powder, and salt. In another bowl, whisk together the remaining ingredients. Stir the wet ingredients into the dry ones, stirring until well blended.

Pour the batter into the loaf pan and bake for 1 hour and 20 minutes, or until a toothpick inserted into the center of the loaf comes out clean. Completely cooled bread can be refrigerated for up to 5 days.

Yield: one 9 x 5-inch (23 x 13 cm) loaf

■ BANANA-GINGER QUICK BREAD WITH CHOPPED MACADAMIAS

Dairy-Free, Soy-Free, Vegetarian

This recipe features coconut flour, which has a naturally sweet flavor, yet contains more fiber and less starch than most flours do. That means it's a great flour to use when making less-starchy, less-sugary baked goods. And it's tropical, too, which makes it a natural match for bananas, macadamia nuts, and ginger.

Unrefined macadamia nut oil
  or extra-virgin olive oil, for
  greasing pan
½ cup (42 g) unsweetened flaked
  coconut
½ cup (70 g) coconut flour
½ cup (60 g) buckwheat or sorghum
  flour
½ cup (80 g) millet flour
2 teaspoons (3.6 g) ground dried
  ginger
½ cup (56 g) chopped macadamia
  nuts
2 teaspoons (9 g) baking powder*
Dash of sea salt
2 large ripe bananas, well spotted
  but not blackened
3 eggs*
¼ cup (60 ml) unrefined macadamia
  nut oil or extra-virgin olive oil
¾ cup (175 ml) whole coconut milk
2 tablespoons (40 g) honey, optional
*See Notes on page 41

Preheat the oven to 350°F (180°C, or gas mark 4). Grease a 9 x 5-inch (23 x 13 cm) glass loaf pan with oil.

Spread the flaked coconut in a large skillet. Toast over medium-low heat for 5 minutes, or until the flakes start to turn light brown, stirring occasionally to prevent any hot spots from scorching your coconut. As the flakes toast, they'll become more and more fragrant.

In a medium bowl, whisk together the toasted coconut, flours, ginger, nuts, baking powder, and sea salt. In a large bowl, mash the bananas with a potato masher until smooth. Whisk in the eggs, oil, coconut milk, and honey. Stir the dry ingredients into the wet ingredients, stirring until well blended.

Pour the mixture into the loaf pan and bake for 1 hour, or until a toothpick inserted into the center comes out clean. If the top is browning too quickly after 45 minutes of baking, cover loosely with foil and continue to bake.

Cool the loaf on a wire rack. Leftover bread can be refrigerated for up to 4 days.

Yield: one 9 x 5-inch (23 x 13 cm) loaf

■ FREE-FORM GOAT CHEESE, MILLET & WALNUT SCONES WITH PEARS

Soy-Free, Vegetarian

These scones are flatter than traditional scones—think of them as buttery, savory, oversized breakfast cookies. The combination of cheese, pears, and walnuts creates a sweet-savory blend that'll make you look forward to getting out of bed!

½ cup (45 g) almond flour
½ cup (80 g) millet flour
¼ cup (30 g) raw buckwheat or brown rice flour
1 ½ teaspoons sucanat
½ teaspoon baking powder*
½ teaspoon sea salt
Dash of freshly ground black pepper
¼ cup (30 g) walnuts, chopped

4 tablespoons (55 g) butter*, cold
1 medium pear, skin left on, chopped
2 ounces (55 g) soft goat cheese, herbed if you like*
¼ cup (60 g) plain whole-milk Greek yogurt*
¼ cup (60 ml) whole milk*
2 eggs*, lightly beaten
See Notes on page 41

Preheat the oven to 375°F (190°C, or gas mark 5). Cover a baking sheet with parchment paper and set aside.

In a large bowl, whisk together the flours, sucanat, baking powder, salt, pepper, and walnuts. Cut the butter into small pieces before adding it to the flour mixture. Using a pastry cutter or two forks, cut the butter into the flour.

Stir the chopped pears into the dough and crumble in the soft goat cheese.

Gently stir in the yogurt, milk, and eggs, being carefully not to overblend the bits of goat cheese completely into the dough. (You'll have more end flavor if you have little bursts of goat cheese crumbles in the scones.)

Scoop 8 large spoonfuls of dough onto the covered baking sheets, spacing them equally apart.

Bake for 25 to 30 minutes, or until the tops of the scones are a golden brown and the bottoms are light brown.

Leftover scones can be refrigerated for up to 4 days.

Yield: 8 scones

■ WHOLE-GRAIN PEANUT-CINNAMON PANCAKES

Soy-Free, Vegetarian, 20 minutes or less

No need to miss out on morning flapjacks just because you're gluten-free! Not only are these 'cakes nutritious thanks to their high-protein flours and whole milk, but they're also richly flavored with cinnamon and peanut butter. Top them with a splash of maple syrup and settle in for a delicious whole-grain breakfast.

¾ cup (90 g) buckwheat flour
¾ cup (120 g) amaranth flour
½ cup (80 g) brown rice flour
2 teaspoons (5 g) cinnamon
1 tablespoon (10 g) sucanat or maple sugar
1 tablespoon (14 g) baking powder*
Dash of sea salt

1 ½ cups plus 2 tablespoons (390 ml) whole milk*
1 egg*
⅓ cup (87 g) natural peanut butter
2 teaspoons (10 ml) vanilla extract
Butter, ghee, or unrefined peanut oil, for cooking
Maple syrup and unrefined peanut oil, for serving
See Notes on page 41

In a large bowl, whisk the flours, cinnamon, sucanat, baking powder, and salt until well blended. In a smaller bowl, whisk the milk, egg, peanut butter, and vanilla until well blended. Pour the wet ingredients into the dry ingredients and whisk again just until smooth.

Place a nonstick griddle pan or a large nonstick skillet over medium heat. Drop in a pat of butter and let it melt. Measure ¼ cup (60 ml) batter and pour into pan. The batter will be sticky, so you may need to scoop the batter out of the cup with the edge of a small spatula. The skillet should hold 3 or 4 pancakes at a time.

Cook the pancakes for about 4 minutes, or until there are tiny bubbles forming in the center of each cake and they're turning brown around the edges. Flip each pancake and continue cooking for another 3 minutes, or until golden brown. If you're going to eat all of the pancakes right away, stack them to keep them warm. If you're going to have leftover pancakes, let them cool on a wire rack so they don't get soggy. Serve with twin drizzles of maple syrup and unrefined peanut oil. Leftover pancakes can be refrigerated for up to 5 days.

Yield: about 16 pancakes

■ SAVORY HERBED BUTTERMILK-POTATO WAFFLES

Nut-Free, Soy-Free, Vegetarian

If you're forced to buy a reduced-fat version of buttermilk for this recipe, use 3 ½ cups (830 ml) of buttermilk instead of diluting the 2 cups (470 ml) of buttermilk with 1 ½ cups (355 ml) of water. Whole-milk buttermilk is well worth seeking out—it yields richer, more flavorful waffles. And ice cream and muffins and whatever else you make with buttermilk.

½ cup (80 g) brown rice flour
½ cup (70 g) sorghum flour
½ cup (63 g) corn flour or masa harina*
½ cup (100 g) potato flour (not potato starch)
2 teaspoons (9 g) baking powder*
1 teaspoon baking soda
2 teaspoons (12 g) sea salt
1 tablespoon (3 g) dried Italian herbs

2 cups (470 ml) whole-milk buttermilk*
1 ½ cups (355 ml) water
2 egg whites*
3 whole eggs*
½ cup (112 g) butter, melted*
Coconut oil or melted butter, for greasing the waffle maker
See Notes on page 41

Set your Belgian waffle maker to medium.

Whisk together the flours, baking powder and soda, salt, and herbs in a large bowl. In a separate bowl, whisk together the milk, water, egg whites, eggs, and butter. Stir the wet ingredients into the dry ones, stirring well to combine.

Spoon or brush a little oil onto each indentation of the waffle maker and flip it over to evenly disperse the oil. Scoop about 1 cup (235 ml) of batter onto the maker, using a spatula or knife to scrape out the cup measure if needed. Cook for approximately 7 minutes, or until golden brown.

Use a heatproof spatula and a fork to delicately wiggle the waffle free from the iron. Regrease the iron—flipping to disperse the oil—before doing the next waffle. Grease the iron between each waffle to prevent sticking.

Serve the waffles immediately or let cool on a wire rack. Waffles can be refrigerated for up to 1 week (or frozen for several months) and then reheated in the toaster oven.

Yield: about seven 8-inch (20 cm) Belgian-style waffles

▶ SHRIMP SCRAMBLE WITH CHOPPED AVOCADO & MANGO

Nut-Free, Dairy-Free (use extra-virgin olive oil), Soy-Free, 20 minutes or less

Look for champagne mangoes. They're less than half the size of standard mangoes, but they're sweeter and more flavorful. Champagne mangoes are solidly orange (as opposed to shaded hues of orange and red) and are slightly teardrop-shaped.

1 avocado, flesh only, chopped
1 champagne or other small mango, flesh only, chopped
Spritz of fresh lemon juice
4 eggs*
Handful of chives or 4 green onions, minced

Freshly ground black pepper
½ pound (225 g) medium shrimp (15/20 count), peeled and deveined*
Extra-virgin olive oil or butter for cooking
See Notes on page 41

Gently toss the avocado, mango, and lemon juice in a medium bowl. Set aside. In another bowl, use a fork to gently whisk together the eggs, chives, and pepper. Set aside.

Cut each shrimp into 4 equal pieces. Heat a drizzle of oil or a pat of butter in a large skillet over medium heat for 2 minutes. Add the shrimp and cook for 2 minutes, or until the shrimp are just starting to turn pink and opaque. Pour in the egg mixture and continue to cook, stirring often, for 3 minutes, or until the eggs are softly scrambled—that is, until they're opaque all the way through and are fluffy. Remove the pan from the heat promptly.

Top each portion of shrimp scramble with the chopped avocado and mango mixture before serving. This dish is best enjoyed fresh off the stove!

Yield: 4 servings

■ PB&J TRIPLE-DECKER PANCAKE SANDWICH

Soy-Free, Vegetarian, 20 minutes or less

You can use this triple-decker idea for any pancake or filling that you'd like. If you're doing the classic PB&J, look for natural peanut butter—the ingredient list should read only "peanuts" or "peanuts and salt"—and jam or jelly that's sweetened with fruit, not sugar. Apricot jam tends to be one of the least-sugary options, and it pairs beautifully with peanut butter.

1 batch Whole-Grain Peanut-Cinnamon Pancakes (page 49)

Natural peanut butter
No-sugar-added jam or jelly

Spread a pancake generously with the peanut butter. Stack another on top and spread with the jam. Add a third pancake to make a "triple deck." Talk about an easy breakfast!

Yield: 5 sandwiches

■ BACON, ONION & SPINACH FRITTATA

Nut-Free, Dairy-Free, Soy-Free

French people say "quiche," Spanish say "tortilla," Italians say "frittata." All of them are referring to a similar dish, one that's made chiefly of eggs and features plenty of veggies and sometimes meat. It makes a great breakfast! (Or lunch, or dinner.)

6 strips bacon*
1 small onion, thinly sliced
6 eggs*
1 cup (81 g) frozen chopped spinach
   (See Recipe Note)

Extra-virgin olive oil, for cooking
2 medium red-skin potatoes,
   unpeeled, thinly sliced
*See Notes on page 41

Preheat the oven to 375°F (190°C, or gas mark 5). Line a rimmed baking tray with aluminum foil and set a wire rack on top of the foil. Lay the bacon strips out over the wire rack. Bake uncovered for 20 minutes, or until the bacon is browned and curling along the edges.

Let the bacon cool before lifting the rack out of the baking tray. Carefully pour the rendered grease into a 12-inch (30 cm) skillet. Add the onions and cook over medium-low heat for 7 to 10 minutes, or until the onions are soft and fragrant.

While the onions cook, crack the eggs into a large mixing bowl. Whisk in the spinach. Coarsely chop the cooked bacon and whisk into the eggs. Add the cooked onions.

Using the same skillet (no need to clean), drizzle with oil and arrange the potato slices in a single layer. Cover and cook over medium-low heat for 5 minutes. The potatoes should be tender but not browned. Add the potatoes to the egg mixture.

Add another drizzle of oil to the skillet before adding the egg-potato mixture. Cover and cook for 5 minutes over medium-low heat. To flip the frittata, cut it into quarters and carefully flip over each quarter. As the second side cooks, the quarters will rejoin, becoming one single frittata. Cover again and cook for 5 minutes, or until both sides are golden brown.

Slip the cooked frittata onto a large plate and serve immediately. Leftover frittata can be refrigerated for up to 1 week.

Yield: 4 to 6 servings

Recipe Notes

➤ Look for spinach that's sold as loose chopped bagged spinach, not as a solid brick.

➤ Cooking pastured bacon is not a messy process. Conventional bacon, on the other hand, is injected with brine, and that brine erupts everywhere. Covering conventional bacon with another sheet of foil is somewhat helpful, but starting out with pastured bacon is your best option.

➤ If you prefer, use low-sodium tamari rather than full-strength tamari. Just make sure your tamari is wheat-free!

■ DIRTY (BROWN) RICE & SAUSAGE

Nut-Free, Dairy-Free, Egg-Free

Though soaking your rice isn't necessary, it's a technique you might consider if you want to cut down on cooking time. For instance, if you soak brown rice in water overnight or for at least 6 hours, the rice will cook in about 15 minutes rather than 35 to 40 minutes. Presoaked wild rice will be done in 20 minutes or so; otherwise, it will need about 50 minutes to cook. Should you be lucky enough to get your hands on true wild rice from Minnesota—which is lighter-colored and longer-grained than the cultivated "wild" rice grown in California—it will cook in 20 minutes without any presoaking.

⅔ cup (123 g) brown or wild rice, uncooked
Extra-virgin olive oil, for cooking
1 large onion, chopped
6 stalks celery, chopped
½ teaspoon Aleppo or dash of cayenne pepper
1 teaspoon oregano

1 teaspoon thyme
2 teaspoons (2 g) dried chives
2 teaspoons (5 g) sweet paprika
½ pound (225 g) ground sausage*
2 tablespoons (28 ml) wheat-free tamari (See Recipe Note)
See Notes on page 41

Place the brown rice and 1 ⅓ cups (315 ml) water in a medium pot. Bring to a boil uncovered, then reduce to low, stir well, and cover. Simmer for 40 minutes, or until the rice has absorbed all of the water. If using wild rice, use 2 cups (475 ml) of water and simmer for about 50 minutes. If using true Minnesotan wild rice, use 2 cups (475 ml) water and simmer for about 20 minutes.

While the rice cooks, warm a drizzle of oil in a large skillet over medium heat. Add the onion and celery and cook for 10 minutes, stirring occasionally. Stir in the remaining ingredients and cook for 5 minutes, or until the sausage is done, stirring often.

Stir in the cooked brown or wild rice and serve hot off the stove. Leftover rice and sausage can be refrigerated for up to 4 days.

Yield: 4 servings

CHAPTER 7 | SANDWICHES, WRAPS & PIZZAS: HANDHELD LUNCHES & DINNERS

When you're eating gluten-free, lunch gets a whole lot more interesting. Instead of the standard bland sandwich on white bread, you can enjoy wraps made of lettuce and collards, stacks made of crepes, boats made of romaine, quesadillas made with 100 percent corn tortillas, pizzas made with multiflavored crust. . . once you get started, you'll never run out of ideas.

■ CRAB, AVOCADO & MANGO LETTUCE WRAPS WITH DIJON DRESSING
Nut-Free, Dairy-Free, Soy-Free, Egg-Free, 20 minutes or less

Like walnuts and pecans, macadamia nuts contain lush amounts of unsaturated oil. That means they can easily go rancid, so be sure to purchase your macadamia nuts from a store that keeps them refrigerated and when you get them home, stash them in your fridge.

For the dressing:
2 tablespoons (28 ml) red wine vinegar
1 teaspoon Dijon mustard
3 tablespoons (45 ml) extra-virgin olive oil

For the filling:
1 pound (455 g) canned white lump crabmeat*
5 green onions, green part only, minced
2 champagne mangoes or 1 standard mango, flesh only, chopped
Generous handful of macadamia nuts, chopped

1 avocado, flesh only, chopped
1 small cucumber or half of an English cucumber, chopped

For the wrappers:
4 to 8 large romaine leaves, rinsed and patted dry*
See Notes on page 41

To make the dressing: Whisk the vinegar and Dijon together in a small bowl. Trickle in the oil, whisking constantly. Set aside.

To make the filling: Toss all of the filling ingredients together in a medium bowl. Toss again with the dressing. Cut away the bottom 2 inches (5 cm) of the romaine leaves and discard. Fill each leaf with the crab filling and serve promptly. If you think you're going to have any leftover filling, don't dress it all, and don't toss it with the avocado. Undressed filling and dressing can be refrigerated separately for up to 3 days.

Yield: 4 servings

■ COLLARD-WRAPPED TUNA & HUMMUS ROLLS

Nut-Free, Dairy-Free, Soy-Free, Egg-Free, 20 minutes or less

When it comes to canned goods, look for products sold in BPA-free cans. BPA is a chemical compound often found in can linings, but unfortunately, it's also been linked to a number of health concerns. (The United States, Canada, and the European Union have banned the use of BPA in baby bottles.) The good news? More and more food producers are packaging their canned goods in BPA-free cans.

Recipe Note
....
➤ Tahini is ground sesame seeds. You may also see this labeled as "sesame paste" or "sesame butter."

For the hummus:
2 tablespoons (28 ml) extra-virgin olive oil
4 cloves garlic, sliced
15 ounces (425 g) canned chickpeas, drained*
Juice of ½ lemon
1 tablespoon (15 g) tahini (See Recipe Note)
1 teaspoon cumin
¼ teaspoon sea salt, plus more to taste

For the rolls:
8 large collard leaves
10 ounces (280 g) canned tuna, drained*
8 small radishes, trimmed, thinly sliced
4 medium carrots, cut into matchsticks
1 small cucumber, cut into matchsticks
See Notes on page 41

To make the hummus: Heat the oil in a small skillet over low heat for 1 minute. Add the garlic and sauté for 3 minutes, or until the garlic is fragrant and turning light brown. Remove from the heat and place in a food processor. Add the chickpeas, lemon juice, tahini, cumin, and salt. Blend until smooth, adding a little more oil or a trickle of water if the hummus is still chunky. Blend again. Taste and see if you'd like to add more salt or lemon juice.

To make the rolls: Trim away any ragged edges from the collard leaves. Cut off the bottom 3 inches (7.5 cm) of the tough ribs. Bring a large pot of water to a boil and add the leaves. Cook uncovered for 3 minutes, then promptly remove the leaves with tongs and let drain.

Spread a leaf out on a plate or cutting board and place a spoonful of tuna in the lower third of the leaf. Add radish slices, carrot sticks, cucumber sticks, and a hearty dab of hummus. Fold the bottom of the leaf up onto the filling. Fold in each edge of the leaf and then roll up, turning it over and tucking in the sides until the leaf is a neat package. Place seam-side down. Repeat with the remaining leaves and filling.

Yield: 8 rolls

■ KOREAN-STYLE PORK & CABBAGE ROMAINE BOATS

Nut-Free, Dairy-Free, Egg-Free

You've probably seen toasted sesame oil in the Asian section of your local market. It's darker colored than untoasted sesame oil, and it's also much stronger tasting—it's made from sesame seeds that were toasted before they were pressed to make oil, and that toasting process accentuates the flavor of the seeds. Because it does have a much more pronounced flavor, toasted sesame oil is usually used as a flavoring or garnish rather than a main cooking oil.

Unrefined sesame oil or extra-
  virgin olive oil, for cooking
8 ounces (225 g) button mushrooms,
  sliced
4 green onions, ends trimmed,
  minced
1 small cucumber, ends trimmed,
  chopped
6 cloves garlic, chopped
2 tablespoons (28 ml) rice vinegar
1 tablespoon (15 ml) wheat-free
  tamari
1 tablespoon (15 ml) toasted sesame oil
  (See Recipe Note)

2 teaspoons (3.6 g) ground dried
  ginger
Dash of cayenne or Aleppo pepper
  (or more if you like hot dishes)
1 pound (455 g) ground pork*
Double handful of finely sliced
  cabbage
Handful of bean sprouts, rinsed
  and drained
8 large romaine leaves, rinsed and
  patted dry*
*See Notes on page 41

Drizzle a generous splash of oil into a large skillet over medium-low heat. Add the mushrooms, green onions, cucumber, and garlic. Cook for 8 min-utes, stirring often, until the mushrooms have shrunk to about half of their original size.

Stir in the remaining ingredients except for the romaine. Increase the heat to medium and cook, stirring often to break up the pork into fine pieces, for 5 to 8 minutes, or until the pork is completely cooked through. Remove from the heat.

Spoon the pork mixture into the romaine leaves and serve immediately. Have the toasted sesame oil, tamari, and cayenne pepper on the table as condiments. Leftover pork can be refrigerated for up to 4 days.

Yield: 4 servings

■ SAVORY CHICKPEA CREPES WITH CURRIED CHICKEN

Nut-Free, Soy-Free

For some reason, people are intimidated by the thought of making crepes. In reality, nothing could be simpler. A crepe is simply a pancake with extra liquid. That's it! And nobody is intimidated by pancakes. So perhaps it's best to think of these as Savory Chickpea with-Extra-Milk-Added Pancakes.

For the crepes:
¾ cup (105 g) chickpea flour
1 egg*
¾ cup plus 2 tablespoons (203 ml) whole milk*
½ teaspoon sea salt
½ teaspoon cumin
Butter, for cooking*

For the chicken:
Ghee or butter, for cooking*
1 small yellow onion, chopped
4 cloves garlic, chopped
2 large tomatoes, chopped
1 teaspoon curry powder
Dash of sea salt
1 pound (455 g) boneless, skinless chicken breasts
    or chicken thighs, trimmed and cut into bite-size
    chunks*
¼ cup (60 g) plain whole-milk Greek yogurt*
See Notes on page 41

To make the crepes: Whisk the crepe ingredients together in a large mixing bowl. Place a dab of butter in a 6-inch (15 cm) nonstick skillet and melt over medium heat. Pour in a scant ¼ cup (60 ml) crepe batter, swirl to cover the bottom of the pan, and cook for 2 to 3 minutes, or until the crepe is bubbling slightly on top and is browned on the bottom. Flip over the crepe and cook the second side for another 2 minutes, or until both sides are slightly brown. (Occasionally whisk the batter to prevent it from separating.) Use 2 skillets if you'd like to speed things along.

Place the cooked crepe on a wire rack. Make a second crepe in the same skillet(s) using the same technique. Add a fresh dab of butter to the skillet(s) after every third crepe.

To make the chicken: Heat a generous dab of ghee in a large skillet over medium heat until melted. Add the onion and cook, stirring occasionally, for 5 minutes, or until the onion is soft and fragrant. Stir in the garlic, tomatoes, curry powder, and salt. Reduce the heat to medium-low and simmer for 5 minutes.

Stir in the chicken and increase the heat to medium. Cook, stirring often to evenly cook the chicken pieces, for 4 minutes, or until the thickest piece of chicken is opaque when cut in half. Remove from the heat and stir in the yogurt. Serve atop the savory crepes. Leftover chicken and crepes can be refrigerated separately for up to 4 days.

Yield: 4 servings (with 2 extra crepes)

◼ OPEN-FACED TEN-MINUTE FISH TACOS

Nut-Free, Soy-Free, Egg-Free, 20 minutes or less

If you've spent much time in Southern California, you know that fish tacos are the norm. As well they should be! Fish has a lighter flavor that allows the flavor of fresh toppings to shine through. Any firm-fleshed fish makes great tacos.

1 pound (455 g) haddock or other firm-fleshed fish,
   with or without skin*
Extra-virgin olive oil, for cooking
Juice of 1 lime
Wedge of cabbage, for garnish

Monterey Jack or other mild cheese, for garnish*
1 avocado
Fresh-style salsa, either homemade or store-bought
4 whole-grain 100% corn tortillas*
See Notes on page 41

Rinse the fish under cold running water and pat dry. If necessary, cut the fillet in half to fit into the skillet you'll be using. Heat a drizzle of oil in a large nonstick skillet over medium heat. Lay the fish fillets in the skillet with the skin-side up. Cover and cook for 4 minutes. Gently flip each fillet over and reduce the heat to low. Pour in the lime juice, cover the skillet, and cook 2 to 3 minutes, or until the fish is opaque and flakes cleanly when you twist the tines of a fork into the thickest part of the fish. Remove to a plate.

Cut the cabbage into thin slices and shred the cheese, placing each into its own bowl. To prep the avocado, cut it in half around the pit, then pull apart. To remove the pit, carefully thunk a large chef's knife into the pit. Twist gently and pull up to remove the pit. Grab the pit with a paper towel and wiggle it free from the knife, being very careful to pull away from the knife. Discard the pit. Cut each avocado in half again to make quarters, then peel away the skin, working with one quarter at a time. Chop the avocado flesh into rough cubes and place in its own bowl.

Heat the tortillas by placing them in a dry skillet over medium heat, then toasting them for about 2 minutes on each side or until the tortillas are fragrant and stiff but not browned. While the tortillas are toasting, remove the skin from the cooked fish (if necessary) by scraping away the skin with the edge of a knife. Coarsely cut the fish into pieces.

Top each tortilla with fish and all the toppings. Fresh, simple, and easy—this is authentic Mexican fare!

Yield: 4 tacos

STACKED CREPE TORTE WITH WILD SALMON

Nut-Free, Soy-Free, Egg-Free

Because whole-milk Greek yogurt is so deliciously thick, it makes richly satisfying dips, dressings, and fillings. In this dish, its full-fledged flavor is the ideal partner for wild salmon's assertive nature.

For the salmon filling:
8 ounces (225 g) smoked wild salmon*
Juice of 1 lemon
4 green onions, green part only, roughly chopped
2 teaspoons (2 g) dried dill
¼ cup (34 g) drained capers
¾ cup (180 g) plain whole-milk Greek yogurt*

For the crepes:
½ cup (70 g) sorghum flour
½ cup (80 g) brown rice flour
1 ½ cups (355 ml) whole milk*
2 eggs*
Butter, for cooking*

1 small cucumber or ½ English cucumber,
   sliced paper-thin
See Notes on page 41

To make the filling: Place all the ingredients in a food processor. Blend until smooth, occasionally scraping down the sides. Transfer the filling to a bowl.

   To make the crepes: Whisk the ingredients together in a large mixing bowl. Place a dab of butter in a 6-inch (15 cm) nonstick skillet and melt over medium heat. Pour in a scant ¼ cup (60 ml) crepe batter, swirl to cover the bottom of the pan, and cook for 2 to 3 minutes, or until the crepe is bubbling slightly on top and is browned on the bottom. Flip over the crepe and cook the second side for another 2 minutes or until both sides are slightly brown. (Occasionally whisk the batter to prevent it from separating.) Use 2 skillets if you'd like to speed things along.

   Place the cooked crepe on a wire rack. Make a second crepe in the same skillet(s) using the same technique. Add a fresh dab of butter to the skillet(s) after every third crepe.

   When the crepes are cool to the touch, place the largest one on a plate. Spread with about one-tenth of the filling and cover with a layer of cucumber. Add the next crepe and repeat, spreading the filling evenly across each crepe to create a stable torte, until you've reached the top. Don't spread any filling on the topmost crepe, and save the prettiest crepe to put on top.

   Cut the torte into 4 or 6 slices with a gentle sawing motion. (Pressing down with a dull knife will push out the filling and smash the torte.) Leftover torte can be refrigerated for up to 3 days.

Yield: one 12-crepe-tall torte; 4 or 6 servings

■ MOROCCAN QUESADILLAS

Nut-Free, Soy-Free, Egg-Free, Vegetarian, 20 minutes or less

You can usually find preblended za'atar at well-stocked spice shops and grocery stores specializing in Middle Eastern ingredients. If you can't find it preblended, though, it's easy enough to make your own. Za'atar is a much-loved spice throughout the Middle East and is often featured in dishes with an Arabic origin. Mixed with a dab of extra-virgin olive oil, za'atar also makes a delightful dip and salad dressing.

For the za'atar:
1 tablespoon (8 g) sesame seeds
1 ½ teaspoons oregano
1 ½ teaspoons thyme
½ teaspoon sea salt
1 tablespoon (7 g) ground sumac
(See Recipe Note)

For the quesadillas:
8 whole-grain 100% corn tortillas*
About 2 cups (about 260 g) total of mixed roasted vegetables: carrots, red pepper, zucchini, or onion are all great choices (see page 79)
4 ounces (115 g) feta cheese, crumbled or chopped (See Recipe Note)
Sautéed or grilled chicken or lamb*, optional
See Notes on page 41

To make the za'atar: Measure the spices into a clean spice jar and shake well. Store the unused portion in a cool, dark place for future use.

To make the quesadillas: Place a tortilla in a large nonstick pan over medium heat and dry-toast for 2 minutes, or until the tortilla begins to turn crispy and brown. Remove from the pan. Repeat with 3 more tortillas.

On a large plate or cutting board, top one of the uncooked tortillas with about ½ cup (65 g) of vegetables, a layer of cheese, and meat. Sprinkle on at least ½ teaspoon za'atar and another layer of cheese.

Carefully lay the tortilla with the toppings in the hot pan, place a browned tortilla browned-side-up on top, press down lightly, and put a lid on the pan. Let cook, shaking the pan slightly to prevent the quesadilla from sticking, for 2 to 3 minutes, or until the bottom has browned and the cheese has begun to melt. (Use a spatula to lift up the bottom edge to check on its progress.) Remove to an empty skillet and cover to keep warm. Repeat with the remaining 3 tortillas for a total of 4 filled quesadillas. Use kitchen shears to cut each quesadilla into quarters. Serve immediately.

Yield: 4 quesadillas

Recipe Note

> For an interesting variation, sprinkle a little cinnamon onto the Brie before heating the quesadillas. Doing so will make the dish more dessert-like.

■ BRIE & PEAR QUESADILLAS

Nut-Free, Soy-Free, Egg-Free, Vegetarian, 20 minutes or less

Ah . . . fruit and cheese. It's a classic pairing. Here, we match Brie with pears, but you could just as easily opt for Cheddar and apples or soft goat cheese and strawberries. That's the beauty of this recipe—just keep switching partners, and you'll always have a new dish to try!

2 firm Bosc pears
Juice of ½ lemon
Brie, Camembert, or other soft-rind,
  creamy cheese*

8 whole-grain 100% corn tortillas*
See Notes on page 41

Core the pears and cut them into thin slices. Toss with the lemon juice and enough water to make it easy to coat the pears. Cut the Brie into wedges or slices. This is easiest if the Brie is well chilled.

Place a tortilla in a large nonstick pan over medium heat and dry-toast for 2 minutes, or until the tortilla is beginning to turn crispy and brown. Remove from the pan. Repeat with 3 more tortillas.

On a large plate or cutting board, top one of the uncooked tortillas with a layer of cheese, one-quarter of the sliced pears, and another layer of cheese.

Carefully lay the tortilla with toppings in the hot pan, place a browned tortilla browned-side-up on top, press down lightly, and put a lid on the pan. Let cook, shaking the pan slightly to prevent the quesadilla from sticking, for 2 to 3 minutes, or until the bottom has browned and the cheese has begun to melt. (Use a spatula to lift up the bottom edge to check on its progress.) Remove to an empty skillet and cover to keep warm. Repeat with the 3 remaining uncooked tortillas to make a total of 4 filled quesadillas. Use kitchen shears to cut each quesadilla into quarters while warm. Serve immediately.

Yield: 4 quesadillas

■ OPEN-FACED BLT ON A SAVORY PANCAKE

Nut-Free, Soy-Free, 20 minutes or less

Coffee grinders are flour mills, too! The typical grinder can grind up to 1 cup (160 g) of flour at once. Extremely hard grains such as buckwheat and brown rice are too hard for coffee grinders to pulverize, but it only takes a few seconds to grind softer grains, including quinoa, rolled oats, amaranth, and teff. Try grinding your own quinoa flour for these pancakes!

For the pancakes:
⅓ cup (39 g) quinoa flour
⅓ cup (48 g) fava bean or
   chickpea flour
⅓ cup (45 g) masa harina
½ teaspoon sea salt
½ teaspoon baking powder
1 egg*
¾ cup (175 ml) whole milk*
Butter, for cooking*

For the BLT toppings:
Stone-ground Dijon mustard
Slight drizzle of honey if you'd like
   a touch of contrasting sweetness,
   optional
8 slices cooked bacon* (see page
   55 for cooking instructions)
1 large ripe tomato, thinly sliced
4 romaine leaves, torn into bite-
   size pieces
See Notes on page 41

To make the pancakes: Whisk the flours with the sea salt and baking powder in a large bowl. Add the egg and milk and whisk until smooth. Heat a dab of butter in a griddle pan or large skillet over medium-low heat until melted. Add batter to the pan in scant ¼ cupfuls (60 ml). You'll probably need to do 2 batches to avoid crowding the pan.

Cook the pancakes for 4 to 5 minutes, or until bubbles form in the center and the bottom is golden brown. Flip and cook another 3 minutes, or until the second side is also golden brown. Stack the finished cakes on a plate to keep them warm.

To top the BLTs: Spread a thin layer of Dijon onto 4 pancakes. If you like, add a tiny drizzle of honey and spread that thinly, too. Tear each bacon strip in half. Top each of the cakes with 4 half-strips of bacon, alternating them with slices of tomato and pieces of romaine. Serve promptly.

Yield: 4 servings (makes 2 extra pancakes)

Recipe Note

➤ Masa harina is a special type of corn flour used to make tortillas. Its fine-grained texture and ability to stick together without being dense also creates fluffy, savory pancakes—not surprising, considering that tortillas and pancakes are both classic flatbreads, one from Central/South America and the other from North America.

■ GOAT CHEESE, FIG & CARAMELIZED ONION PIZZA

Nut-Free, Soy-Free, Egg-Free, Vegetarian

If you use dried figs for this pizza topping, soak them in hot water for at least 20 minutes and then drain before roughly chopping. Rehydrating the figs will make them easier to chop and will also give them a creamy texture as they bake into the onion- and cheese-topped crust.

For the toppings:
1 large sweet onion, thinly sliced
Extra-virgin olive oil, for cooking and oiling the pan
4 cloves garlic, chopped
6 fresh figs, quartered, or 10 dried figs
4 ounces (115 g) soft goat cheese, herbed if
   you like*
4 ounces (115 g) goat's-milk Gouda*

For the crust:
½ cup (70 g) chickpea flour
½ cup (80 g) brown rice flour
½ cup (100 g) potato flour (not potato starch)
½ cup (63 g) corn flour* (not cornstarch)
1 ½ teaspoons sea salt
Plenty of freshly ground pepper
1 heaping teaspoon active dry yeast
⅔ cup (160 ml) hot tap water
½ cup (120 ml) whole milk*
See Notes on page 41

To make the topping: Sauté the onion slices in a generous drizzle of oil over medium-low heat, stirring infrequently. They'll caramelize while you make the rest of the dish.

   To make the crust: Preheat the oven to 425°F (220°C, or gas mark 7). Whisk together the dry crust ingredients, then stir in the water and milk. Add more water if the dough is too dry and thick. Rub a round 12-inch (30 cm) aerated pizza pan with oil and then rub your hands with the oil. Press the dough into the pan with your oiled hands, reoiling them if the dough starts to stick to your hands. Bake for 12 minutes, or until the crust starts to brown. Remove from the oven and set aside. Reduce the heat to 400°F (200°C, or gas mark 6).

   Sauté the garlic over medium-low heat with a little oil of its own for 3 minutes, or until the garlic starts to turn golden brown. Stir in the figs and caramelized onions.

   Top the baked crust with the caramelized onions, sautéed garlic, figs, and cheeses. Bake for 15 minutes, or until the cheese is melted and bubbling. Use kitchen shears to cut the hot pizza into 6 or 8 slices.

Yield: one 12-inch (30 cm) round pizza

■ LAMB PIZZA WITH FOUR-GRAIN CRUST

Nut-Free, Soy-Free, Egg-Free

There's nothing wrong with pepperoni and mushrooms, but when it comes to pizza toppings, sometimes it's more fun to play with new ideas. For this Middle Eastern–influenced pie, you'll experiment with adding ingredients such as pine nuts, pepperoncinis, and mint. For a more standard pie, when you make the sauce, swap out the lamb for beef and omit the mint, then use whichever toppings you like.

For the crust:
½ cup (70 g) sorghum or brown rice flour
½ cup (80 g) millet flour
½ cup (80 g) amaranth flour
¾ cup (150 g) teff flour
1 ½ teaspoons sea salt
Plenty of freshly ground pepper
1 heaping teaspoon active dry yeast
½ cup (120 ml) hot tap water
½ cup (120 ml) whole milk or buttermilk*
Extra-virgin olive oil, for oiling the pizza pan

For the lamb sauce:
1 small yellow onion, sliced
½ pound (225 g) ground lamb*
4 cloves garlic, sliced
15 ounces (425 g) diced canned tomatoes
1 teaspoon dried mint
1 teaspoon dried thyme
2 teaspoons (2 g) dried oregano

Additional toppings:
Handful of baby spinach leaves, chopped*
Handful of pine nuts
4 pepperoncinis, seeds and stems removed, sliced
Handful of mild green olives, pitted and chopped
About 1 ½ cups (180 g) grated aged Manchego cheese*
Fresh mint, chopped, for garnish
*See Notes on page 41

To make the crust: Preheat the oven to 425°F (220°C, or gas mark 7). Whisk together the dry crust ingredients, then stir in the water and milk with a spoon or use your hands. Rub a round 12-inch (30 cm) aerated pizza pan with extra-virgin olive oil. Press the dough into the pan with your oiled hands, reoiling them if the dough starts to stick. Bake for 14 minutes or until the crust starts to brown. Remove from the oven and set aside. Reduce the heat to 400°F (200°C, or gas mark 6).

　To make the lamb sauce: Heat the onion, lamb, and garlic in a large skillet over medium-low heat. Cook for 5 minutes or until the lamb is completely browned, stirring occasionally. Add the remaining sauce ingredients and let simmer for 20 minutes, reducing the heat to low if the simmer threatens to become a boil.

　To top the pizza: Top the baked crust with the lamb sauce, then scatter on the spinach leaves, pine nuts, pepperoncinis, and olives. Cover with the grated cheese and bake for 15 minutes, or until the cheese is melted and bubbling. Use kitchen shears to cut the hot pizza into 6 or 8 slices. Garnish with the fresh mint.

Yield: one 12-inch (30 cm) round pizza

CHAPTER 8 | SALADS & PILAFS: CELEBRATING VEGGIES & WHOLE GRAINS

Nothing celebrates the seasons like fresh veggies! And they're the perfect partner for whole grains, especially in pilafs and other grain-based dishes. These recipes will give you plenty of reasons to explore produce markets as well as the grains aisle. More and more farmers' markets feature grains right alongside the veggies, too. You might find amaranth snuggled up with spinach!

■ PEAR, WALNUT & GORGONZOLA SALAD
Soy-Free, Egg-Free, Vegetarian, 20 minutes or less

Blue cheeses get their blue hue from specific molds. Most people can enjoy cheeses from this family, but if you're sensitive to mold, you may want to avoid blue cheese. In that case, substitute an aged hard cheese such as Cheddar, Manchego, or Gruyère—those cheeses also have a sharp, almost tangy flavor that pairs well with firm, sweet pears. Plus, hard cheeses can be grated into attractive shards that look striking perched atop a salad.

For the dressing:
1 tablespoon (15 ml) balsamic vinegar
1 teaspoon thyme
Fresh grind of pepper
3 tablespoons (45 ml) extra-virgin olive oil

For the salad:
½ red onion, thinly sliced
¾ cup (75 g) walnut halves
1 head romaine lettuce, bottom ends trimmed,
    roughly chopped*
2 ripe but firm Bosc pears, cored and chopped
Gorgonzola or your favorite blue cheese, for garnish*
*See Notes on page 41

To make the dressing: Place the all ingredients in a small glass jar with a lid. Close tightly and shake well. Set aside.

To make the salad: Rinse the onion slices under cold running water, then place in a bowl of cold water for at least 15 minutes. Drain well. Doing this will wash away some of the sulfuric acid in the onion and will make it less pungent. If you'd rather have a pungent onion flavor, skip this step.

Place the walnuts in a dry skillet over medium-low heat. Toast for about 5 minutes, shaking the skillet occasionally, or until the walnuts are fragrant and turning golden brown. Immediately transfer to a large bowl. Add the chopped romaine, pears, and onions and toss well. Drizzle on the dressing and toss again.

Top each individual portion with the Gorgonzola and serve immediately.

Yield: 4 servings

■ HAND-TORN TORTILLA FATTOUSH WITH CUCUMBER, TOMATOES & MINT

Nut-Free, Dairy-Free, Soy-Free, Egg-Free, 20 minutes or less

For a real treat, try making your own tortilla chips! Cut tortillas into triangles, then fry them in rendered bacon grease over medium-low heat, flipping once or twice, until they get crispy and light brown. (It's best to use tongs to flip them and press them into the grease as they're frying.) Your DIY chips would be delicious in this fattoush, too!

4 whole-grain 100% corn tortillas*
1 English cucumber
6 red radishes
About 12 mint leaves
Romaine or other hearty lettuce*
¼ red onion, thinly sliced
2 or 3 large tomatoes, chopped

1 yellow or red bell pepper, cored, seeded, and chopped
Juice of 1 small lemon or ½ large lemon
2 tablespoons (28 ml) extra-virgin olive oil
Sea salt to taste
Sumac, for garnish, optional
Sautéed or grilled chicken for garnish*, optional
See Notes on page 41

Place the tortillas in a large skillet over medium heat. Dry-toast for several minutes on each side or until the tortillas are fragrant, crispy, and starting to turn golden brown. Set aside.

Prep the veggies, adding each to a large bowl as you go. Trim away the cucumber ends (but do not remove the skin or seeds) and chop. Trim away the ends of the radishes and slice them into thin rounds. Rinse the mint and pat it dry, then roll the leaves into thin tubes and slice thinly to create delicate ribbons. Trim away the ends of the romaine, rinse with cool water, and pat dry. Chop roughly before adding to bowl. Add the onion, tomatoes, and pepper.

Tear the crisped tortillas into bite-size pieces and add to the bowl. Toss well. Drizzle with the lemon juice and oil and toss well again, then add salt to taste. Divide into 4 portions and garnish with the sumac and chicken before serving. It's best to enjoy this dressed salad promptly, while the tortillas are still crisp.

Yield: 4 servings

■ CORNBREAD PANZANELLA WITH MOZZARELLA PEARLS

Nut-Free, Soy-Free, Vegetarian

Mozzarella pearls are tiny balls of mozzarella. They're bite-size, luscious, and flat-out adorable, plus their creaminess contrasts deliciously with other key ingredients of this dish: juicy sweet-tart tomatoes, savory olives, and aromatic basil.

Recipe Note

➤ To chiffonade the basil leaves, rinse them and pat them dry, then roll into tight tubes. Use a very sharp knife to thinly slice the tubes—they'll unroll into thin ribbons.

For the cornbread:
2 tablespoons (28 g) butter*
¾ cup (95 g) corn flour* (not cornstarch)
½ cup (84 g) stone-ground cornmeal* (not degerminated)
1 teaspoon baking powder*
1 teaspoon sea salt
4 eggs*
¾ cup (175 ml) whole milk*

For the panzanella:
¼ red onion, thinly sliced
2 or 3 large tomatoes, chopped
Handful of fresh basil leaves, chiffonade (see Recipe Note)
8 ounces or more (225 g) mozzarella pearls*
12 to 16 pitted green Niçoise olives, chopped, optional
2 tablespoons (28 ml) extra-virgin olive oil
1 tablespoon (15 ml) balsamic vinegar
*See Notes on page 41

To make the cornbread: Preheat the oven to 375°F (190°C, or gas mark 5). Place the butter in a glass 8 x 8-inch (20 x 20 cm) pan and pop it into the oven just long enough to melt the butter.

In a medium bowl, whisk together the corn flour, cornmeal, baking powder, and salt. In a small bowl, whisk together the eggs and milk. Pour the wet ingredients into the dry and whisk until smooth. Pour into the buttered pan and bake for 30 minutes, or until the edges and bottom are golden brown and are pulling away from the pan. Let cool for at least 10 minutes before cutting into the cornbread.

To make the panzanella: Rinse the onion slices under cold running water, then place in a bowl of cold water to soak for at least 15 minutes. Drain well.

Cut about half of the cornbread into bite-size cubes. Place in a large bowl with the onion, tomatoes, basil, mozzarella pearls, and olives. Gently toss with wooden spoons. Drizzle on the oil and vinegar and gently toss again to combine. Serve immediately. Because this salad contains fresh basil and is dressed, it should be eaten promptly. Leftover undressed cornbread can be refrigerated for up to 5 days.

Yield: 4 servings, plus extra cornbread

■ SALADE NIÇOISE

Nut-Free, Soy-Free, 20 minutes or less

This classic salad originally hails from Nice, France. Green beans, hard-boiled eggs, tuna, and olives are its key ingredients. I've added avocado for extra creaminess and feta cheese for a contrasting tanginess.

For the dressing:
¼ cup (60 ml) extra-virgin olive oil
2 tablespoons (28 ml) red wine vinegar
1 teaspoon dried Italian herbs

For the salad:
2 to 4 eggs*
4 medium red-skin potatoes or red fingerling potatoes,
   cut into bite-size pieces
¾ pound (340 g) green beans, trimmed and cut into
   2-inch (5 cm) lengths
Several thin slices red onion
1 avocado, sliced or cubed
10 ounces (280 g) canned tuna*
4 large romaine leaves, chopped*
Generous handful of halved cherry or grape tomatoes
Handful of pitted green or black Niçoise olives, chopped
Handful of feta or blue cheese for garnish*
See Notes on page 41

To make the dressing: Place all the ingredients in a small glass jar with a lid. Close tightly and shake well. Set aside.

   To make the salad: Place the eggs in a medium pot and fill with enough water to cover the eggs. Bring to a boil. As soon as the water boils, cover the pot, reduce the heat to medium-low, and simmer the eggs for 10 minutes. Pour the hot water out of the pot and run cold water into it. Allow the eggs to cool in the cold water for at least 5 minutes before peeling and chopping.

   While the eggs cook, fill another medium pot halfway with water. Bring to a boil and add the potatoes. Reduce the heat to medium and simmer, covered, for 5 minutes. Add the beans and simmer for an additional 5 minutes. Drain well.

   In a large bowl, toss the remaining ingredients except the cheese with the chopped hard-boiled eggs, the cooked veggies, and the dressing. Garnish individual plates with the feta before serving. Leftover undressed salad—sans the avocado—can be refrigerated for up to 3 days.

Yield: 4 servings

■ ROASTED VEGGIES WITH FETA

Nut-Free (use olive oil), Soy-Free, Egg-Free, Vegetarian

Roasting veggies is so easy—just toss with oil and bake. And the best part is that you can use your leftover veggies in anything from omelets to soups to salads.

Any vegetable you like: bell peppers, onions, cherry/grape tomatoes, eggplants, green beans, squash, beets, sweet potatoes, mushrooms, corn kernels, etc.

Unrefined peanut oil or extra-virgin olive oil, for roasting
Sea salt and freshly ground pepper
Feta cheese, preferably made with sheep and/or goat's milk*
See Notes on page 41

Preheat the oven to 375°F (190°C, or gas mark 5). Prep the veggies by rinsing them and then peeling them if necessary. Cut larger veggies into ¼-inch-thick (6 mm) slices. Smaller, thinner veggies such as green beans and corn kernels are fine just the way they are.

Cover 1 or 2 large baking trays with parchment paper and place the veggies on the trays, keeping the same veggies grouped together. Drizzle lightly with the oil and sprinkle with the sea salt and freshly ground pepper. Flip and push the veggies around to make sure they're evenly coated.

Baking time will depend greatly on which veggies you use. Start checking the oven at about 25 minutes and pull out the veggies as needed, leaving the thicker/larger ones in the oven until they're also turning brown around the edges and have become slightly shriveled.

Crumble or chop the feta and toss with the veggies. Leftovers can be refrigerated for up to 5 days.

Yield: Varies based on amount used.

ROASTED GARLIC

When roasted, garlic transforms from pungent and arresting to smooth and nutty. Store leftovers in the fridge for up to a week.

Preheat the oven to 400°F (200°C, or gas mark 6). Cut off the very top of a head of garlic and place the head on a large square of aluminum foil. Drizzle a bit of extra-virgin olive oil on the top and sprinkle with sea salt and freshly ground pepper. Fold the foil to cover the garlic and place in the oven. Roast for 45 minutes.

Let the garlic cool until it has reached room temperature, then squeeze out the contents of the entire head onto a plate, pushing from the root outward and leaving the papery part behind. The garlic will be very sticky! (This is why it's important for the garlic to be at room temperature.) If you want to save some of the garlic for later, squeeze out only a few of the cloves. Store roasted garlic cloves in a glass jar in the refrigerator for up to 1 week.

▶ SALTY-SWEET HALLOUMI & GRAPE SALAD

Nut-Free, Soy-Free, Egg-Free, Vegetarian, 20 minutes or less

Many Greek cheeses fall into the category of "fry cheese," like the kasseri that's used for the flaming cheese dish most Americans know as "saganaki." (Or "opa" because often the waiters shout "Opa!" when the flames start shooting up.) Halloumi is another one of Greece's frying cheeses.

For the dressing:
⅓ cup (80 ml) extra-virgin olive oil
2 tablespoons (28 ml) balsamic
   vinegar
1 teaspoon dried basil
1 tablespoon (15 g) Dijon mustard

For the salad:
Several handfuls mixed salad greens*
2 cups (300 g) red grapes, halved*
8 ounces (225 g) halloumi cheese*
See Notes on page 41

To make the dressing: Place all the ingredients in a small glass jar with a lid. Close tightly and shake well. Set aside.

To make the salad: Toss the greens and grapes in a large bowl. Cut the halloumi into slices, then place in a large skillet and fry over medium-high heat. Keep a close eye on the cheese—although its firm texture will prevent it from oozing, halloumi cooks in 4 to 5 minutes. As soon as the slices turn golden brown and look firm and dry, flip them over to brown the other side. Cut into bite-size pieces.

Toss the warm halloumi with the greens, grapes, and dressing. Serve promptly.

Yield: 4 servings

■ MOM'S CAESAR SALAD

Nut-Free, Egg-Free, Vegetarian, 20 minutes or less (if you don't presoak the garlic)

Caesar dressing's signature savoriness comes from anchovies, mustard, and garlic. American renditions also generally include Worcestershire sauce, but because that's typically made with high-fructose corn syrup, I've omitted it in favor of wheat-free tamari and pomegranate molasses, which lend the dressing a similar salty-tangy flavor.

For the dressing:
1 clove garlic, halved
⅓ cup (80 ml) extra-virgin olive oil
½ teaspoon dry mustard
Several grinds of black pepper
5 anchovy fillets
2 tablespoons (28 ml) red wine vinegar
2 tablespoons (28 ml) lemon juice
1 teaspoon wheat-free tamari
1 teaspoon pomegranate molasses

For the salad:
Romaine lettuce, roughly chopped*
Grated or shaved Parmesan*
Baked mochi cubes for croutons (see page 125)
Chopped cooked chicken*, optional
Cooked shrimp*, optional
See Notes on page 41

To make the dressing: Soak the garlic in the oil overnight. Remove before serving. (If you want your Caesar to be extra-garlicky, blend the garlic into the dressing.) Place the remaining ingredients in a food processor and process until well blended. Trickle in the oil with the processor running to create a smooth, emulsified dressing.

To make the salad: Place the salad ingredients and dressing in a large bowl and toss well. Serve immediately. Leftover dressing can be refrigerated separately for up to 1 week.

Yield: 4 servings

DRESSING COLLECTION: MEDITERRANEAN BALSAMIC, ASIAN, AND DILLED YOGURT

Salad dressings are the number one item to make, not buy—whereas commercial dressings are made with refined oils that are flavorless as well as unhealthy, you can make your own dressings in a matter of minutes with fresh, unrefined oils and a variety of herbs and vinegars. It's as simple as pour, whisk, and drizzle!

■ MEDITERRANEAN BALSAMIC DRESSING

Nut-Free, Dairy-Free, Soy-Free, Egg-Free, Vegetarian, 20 minutes or less

3 tablespoons (45 ml) balsamic vinegar
1 teaspoon dried oregano
2 teaspoons (10 g) Dijon mustard

Sea salt and freshly ground pepper
¼ cup (60 ml) extra-virgin olive oil

In a small bowl, whisk the balsamic vinegar with the dried oregano and Dijon. Add a dash of sea salt and a few grinds of fresh pepper and whisk again. Slowly drizzle and whisk in the olive oil. The dressing can be refrigerated for up to 4 days.

Yield: about ½ cup (60 ml)

■ ASIAN DRESSING

Nut-Free, Dairy-Free, Egg-Free, Vegetarian, 20 minutes or less

3 tablespoons (45 ml) unrefined
    sesame oil
1 tablespoon (15 ml) wheat-free tamari
1 tablespoon (15 ml) fresh orange
    juice

1 tablespoon (15 ml) rice vinegar
1 teaspoon honey
½ teaspoon ginger
1 small clove garlic, minced

Whisk all the ingredients together in a small bowl. If possible, prepare the dressing an hour ahead to give the flavors time to marry. The dressing can be refrigerated for up to 4 days.

Yield: about ⅓ cup (45 ml)

■ DILLED YOGURT DRESSING

Nut-Free, Soy-Free, Egg-Free, Vegetarian, 20 minutes or less

¼ cup (60 g) plain whole-milk
    Greek yogurt*
2 teaspoons (10 ml) fresh lemon juice
2 teaspoons (2 g) dried or fresh
    minced chives

1 teaspoon dried or fresh minced dill
2 teaspoons (10 ml) extra-virgin
    olive oil
Sea salt and pepper to taste
See Notes on page 41

Whisk together the ingredients in a small bowl. If the dressing is too thick to pour, add 1 teaspoon of water and whisk again.

Yield: about ⅓ cup (80 ml)

■ MOROCCAN MILLET COUSCOUS WITH CHICKEN, OLIVES & LEMON

Nut-Free, Dairy-Free, Soy-Free, Egg-Free

Couscous is made by rolling up tiny balls of semolina flour. Because semolina is a type of wheat, traditional couscous is not on the menu for gluten-free folks. In terms of appearance and flavor, though, millet is a close match—whenever you see couscous called for in a recipe, swap it for millet.

¾ cup (150 g) raw millet
1 ½ cups (355 ml) water
Extra-virgin olive oil, for tossing with the millet
   and for cooking
2 medium carrots, sliced into thin rounds
2 celery stalks, minced
1 small onion, sliced
1 small zucchini, chopped
5 cloves garlic, chopped
¼ pound (115 g) pitted green Niçoise olives, chopped

2 teaspoons (4 g) ground coriander
2 teaspoons (5 g) cumin
Dash of sea salt
1 pound (455 g) trimmed chicken breast, cut into
   ½-inch-thick (1.3-cm) slices*
15 ounces (425 g) canned chickpeas, drained*
Juice and zest of 1 lemon*
¼ cup (60 ml) chicken broth or water*
Sumac or sweet paprika for garnish
See Notes on page 41

Place the millet and water into a pot. Bring to a boil, then reduce the heat to low. Cover and simmer for 20 minutes, or until the millet looks fluffy and is tooth-tender. Drain if necessary. Fluff with a fork, toss with a drizzle of oil, and set aside.

Heat a generous drizzle of oil in a large skillet over medium heat. Add the carrots, celery, and onion and cook for 8 minutes, or until the onions turn translucent, stirring occasionally. Stir in the zucchini, garlic, olives, and spices. Cook undisturbed for another 8 minutes, or until the zucchini and carrots are lightly browned on the bottom. I use this time to prep the chicken.

Stir the remaining ingredients except the garnish into the veggie mixture. Cover and cook for 5 minutes. Flip over the chicken pieces, cover again, and cook an additional 3 minutes, or until the thickest piece of chicken is opaque all the way through. Free-range chicken cooks much more quickly than conventional chicken does—it's leaner—so if you're using conventional chicken, you'll have to cook the chicken for at least 5 minutes on each side. Toss the cooked millet with the chicken and veggies in a large bowl.

When serving, sprinkle on a dash of sumac—the bright red accent will make the dish even more eye-catching. Leftover couscous can be refrigerated for up to 4 days.

Yield: 4 to 6 servings

■ BUCKWHEAT TABBOULEH

Nut-Free, Dairy-Free, Soy-Free, Egg-Free, Vegetarian

The difference between kasha and buckwheat is simple: Kasha is roasted buckwheat, and it has a much stronger taste. Sometimes that's a good thing, but sometimes that stronger flavor can interfere with the rest of the dish. I prefer raw buckwheat, especially in this tabbouleh—you want the brightness of the fresh veggies and herbs to be the stars of the show.

2 ¼ (530 ml) cups water
¾ cup (144 g) raw buckwheat groats
¼ red onion, sliced thinly
1 large seedless orange
2 large tomatoes, chopped
Handful of fresh whole cilantro or parsley leaves (See Recipe Note)
½ handful of fresh mint leaves, torn into small pieces
Juice of ½ lemon
1 tablespoon (15 ml) extra-virgin olive oil
Sea salt and freshly cracked black pepper to taste

Recipe Note

....

➤ Parsley would be a more authentic herb to use in this recipe, but I find that cilantro gives the tabbouleh a smoother flavor. Use whichever you prefer.

Bring the water to a boil. Add the buckwheat and reduce the heat to low. Cover and cook for 15 to 20 minutes, or until the buckwheat has reached its desired tenderness. If the buckwheat hasn't completely absorbed the water but is tender, drain well.

While the buckwheat cooks, rinse the red onion slices and submerge them in a bowl of cool water. This will blunt their sharp taste and will make for more balanced tabbouleh.

Place the orange on a cutting board and slice off both ends. Cut along the curve of the orange right beneath the white pith, shearing off the zest and pith. (If you like, save the zest to put into your water glass. Aromatic orange-infused water is the perfect beverage to serve with this meal!) Chop the orange into small pieces.

In a large bowl, toss the remaining ingredients. Add the cooked buckwheat and toss again. Drain the red onion slices, mince, and toss into the salad. Taste it to see if you'd like to add more salt, pepper, lemon juice, or fresh herbs.

Serve at room temperature. Leftover tabbouleh can be refrigerated for up to 2 days, although for best taste be sure to allow it to come back to room temperature before serving it.

Yield: 4 servings

■ SOUTH-OF-THE-BORDER QUINOA BOWL

Nut-Free, Dairy-Free (omit cheese), Soy-Free, Egg-Free, Vegetarian, 20 minutes or less

Beans and rice are a classic Latin American combo. For this dish, we're upping the nutritional ante by swapping out the rice for quinoa, which is a complete protein. Quinoa and amaranth—both grains from South America—are two of the few plants that can boast being complete proteins. Quinoa is available in tan, red, and black varieties. Their flavors are very similar, but the red and black versions of quinoa offer more micronutrients in the form of their pigments. That old saying about "eat the rainbow" is true—the same phytochemicals responsible for creating the colors are also nutritionally useful. And pretty on our plates!

For the dressing:
¼ cup (60 ml) fresh lime juice
2 tablespoons (28 ml) extra-virgin olive oil
1 tablespoon (7.5 g) chili powder
1 teaspoon cumin
Pinch of sea salt

For the salad:
1 cup (170 g) raw quinoa, rinsed
2 cups (475 ml) vegetable broth
2 cups (454 g) frozen corn, thawed*
15 ounces (425 g) canned black beans, drained*

1 red bell pepper, cored, seeded, and chopped
2 large tomatoes, chopped
4 green onions, green part only, minced

Optional toppings:
Chopped avocado
Fresh mozzarella balls or feta made with sheep
   and/or goat's milk*
Sautéed chicken*
Sautéed shrimp*
See Notes on page 41

To make the dressing: Place all the ingredients in a small glass jar with a lid and shake well.

To make the salad: Place the quinoa and broth in a medium pot and bring to a boil. Immediately reduce the heat to medium-low and simmer, stirring occasionally, for 10 minutes. If any liquid remains after the quinoa has "uncurled"—you'll see their cute little tails form curlicues—drain the quinoa.

Toss the corn, beans, pepper, tomatoes, green onions, and cooked quinoa in a large bowl. Toss again with the dressing and add the optional toppings if desired. Leftovers without avocado can be refrigerated for up to 3 days.

Yield: 4 servings

■ PAELLA WITH SHRIMP & BACON

Nut-Free, Dairy-Free, Soy-Free, Egg-Free

If you're ever in Spain, be on the lookout for paella pans. Some of them are 3 feet (1 m) across! This dish was originally made over a large fire and served dozens of people. Luckily, you can make one of Spain's most famous dishes in your own kitchen. The trick is keeping an eye on the simmering rice to make sure it doesn't dry out—if the paella looks like the liquid will be gone before the rice is tender, pour in another splash of broth or wine.

8 to 10 ounces (225 to 280 g) bacon*
Extra-virgin olive oil (preferably Spanish), for cooking
2 red or yellow bell peppers, cored, seeded, and thinly sliced
1 large yellow onion, thinly sliced
4 cloves garlic, chopped
28 ounces (795 g) crushed canned tomatoes
1 cup (235 ml) free-range chicken broth, vegetable broth, or dry white wine

1 ½ teaspoons cumin
1 ½ teaspoons coriander
Pinch of saffron threads, optional (but adds a classic color and flavor)
1 ½ cups (285 g) raw short-grain brown rice
¾ pound (340 g) shrimp, peeled and deveined*
See Notes on page 41

Prepare the bacon according to instructions on page 55. Let the bacon cool before lifting the rack out of the baking tray. Carefully pour the rendered grease into a waiting shallow glass jar and refrigerate for future use. When the bacon is cool enough to touch, roughly chop it.

While the bacon cooks, start preparing the paella. Drizzle a generous portion of oil into a large skillet. Add the peppers and onions and cook over medium heat for 5 minutes, or until the onions start to turn translucent. Stir in the garlic and cook for another 3 minutes, stirring occasionally.

Stir in the tomatoes, broth, spices, and rice. Reduce the heat to medium-low and cover the skillet. Let simmer for 40 minutes, stirring occasionally, or until the rice has reached the desired tenderness. Bring the heat back up to medium and stir in the bacon and shrimp. Cook, occasionally flipping over the shrimp, for another 3 minutes or until the shrimp have curled and turned pink. Serve immediately. Leftover paella can be refrigerated for up to 2 days.

Yield: 6 servings

CHAPTER 9 | SIMPLE & SATISFYING MEALS: SAUTÉS, PASTAS, SOUPS & STEWS

Most of the recipes in this chapter can be made with a single pot or pan, and all of them are easy to prepare. Plus, hearty stews, quick stir-fries, and savory pasta dishes are ideal for exploring the wide world of whole grains—from buckwheat to wild rice, you'll get a taste of their endless possibilities.

■ PARMESAN-BATTERED FISH & CHIPS

Soy-Free

Like almond flour, grated Parmesan also makes a great coating in lieu of bread crumbs. In this recipe, we're combining the two. Parmesan has the added advantage of forming a slightly crispy, golden brown "crust" coating, plus Parmesan is so savory that you won't need to add any salt to your dish. For an Italian twist on this dish, look for imported Parmigiano-Reggiano—it has a sharper, more pronounced flavor.

2 pounds (905 g) red-skinned or fingerling potatoes
Extra-virgin olive oil, for drizzling
Dash of sea salt
Sprinkling of freshly ground black pepper
1 egg*
½ cup (45 g) freshly ground almonds (run sliced or slivered almonds through a coffee/spice grinder)

½ cup (50 g) grated Parmesan cheese*
1 ½ pounds (680 g) skinless trout, perch, or other mild white fish fillets*
Generous pat of butter, for cooking*
Lemon wedges, for serving
See Notes on page 41

Preheat the oven to 375°F (190°C, or gas mark 5) and cover 2 baking sheets with parchment paper. Cut the potatoes into ½-inch-thick (1.3 cm) slices (if they're fingerlings, cut them lengthwise) and lay on the baking sheets. Drizzle with the oil and toss with the salt and pepper. Roast for 20 to 30 minutes, or until the potatoes are crispy and brown.

In a flat-bottomed bowl, lightly scramble the egg with a fork. Place the almonds and Parmesan in another flat-bottomed bowl (or on a plate) and mix well with your fingertips. Dip a fillet in the egg, shake slightly, and then press into the almond mixture. Place on a clean plate or tray, then repeat with the remaining fillets.

Melt the butter in a large skillet over medium heat. Sauté the fish in the butter for 3 minutes per side, or until the Parmesan is golden brown and the fish flakes cleanly when pierced with a fork. Serve with a side of roasted potatoes and a lemon wedge.

Yield: 4 servings

■ PAN-FRIED WILD SALMON WITH STRAWBERRY SALSA

Nut-Free, Soy-Free, Egg-Free, 20 minutes or less

When you're shopping for salmon—whether fresh or frozen—be sure to choose wild salmon. Most of the nutritional benefits of salmon come from the krill they eat (which is also what gives salmon its distinctive color), and because farmed salmon don't eat krill, they don't offer the same nutritional benefits. In fact, if farmed salmon weren't fed pink dye chips, their flesh would be gray. Wild salmon, on the other hand, ranges in color from orange-pink to ruby-red, and it offers lots of anti-inflammatory omega-3 fats along with better flavor.

For the salsa:
10 medium strawberries, stems removed, chopped*
Juice of 1 lime
5 green onions, green part only, minced
1 clove garlic, minced
Handful of cilantro leaves, chopped
Pinch of sea salt
A few grinds of fresh pepper

For the salmon:
Generous pat of butter, for cooking*
1 ½ pounds (680 g) wild salmon fillets, rinsed and patted dry*
See Notes on page 41

To make the salsa: Combine all the ingredients in a medium bowl. Toss well.

To make the salmon: Heat the butter in a large skillet over medium heat until the butter is bubbling. Place the salmon fillets skin-side up in the butter. Cover the pan and cook for 5 minutes, or until the fillets are opaque halfway up. (Stand well away from the skillet when you lift the lid to check the salmon.) Carefully flip over the fillets, reduce the heat to medium-low, and cook for 4 minutes, or until the salmon flakes easily at the thickest part and is opaque all the way through.

Remove from the heat promptly and serve the salmon with the strawberry salsa. Leftover salmon and salsa can be refrigerated separately for up to 2 days. This makes a great breakfast, too!

Yield: 4 servings

Recipe Note

➤ Because the strongest muscles in any fish are near the tail, the "tail half" of the salmon has more flavor than the "head half" does. If you prefer a more pronounced salmon flavor, when the fishmonger asks whether you'd like the head or the tail, choose the tail. For a more mellow salmon experience, choose a fillet cut from the upper half of the salmon.

■ ALMOND-DUSTED CRAB CAKES

Soy-Free

Almond flour is an easy stand-in for bread crumbs. It's also tastier and more moist than bread crumbs. If you have an inexpensive coffee/spice grinder, you can make your own almond flour. DIY flour is fresher, more nutritious, and much less expensive—typically, home-ground almond flour costs half as much as store-bought almond flour. Those ten seconds of grinding can save you a lot of money!

For the sauce:
¼ cup (60 g) Dijon mustard
¼ cup (60 g) plain whole-milk Greek yogurt*

For the cakes:
1 pound (455 g) canned lump white crabmeat*
1 tablespoon (10 g) minced green onion,
   green part only
1 teaspoon Dijon mustard
½ teaspoon ground mustard
1 teaspoon dried dill or 2 teaspoons (2.6 g) fresh dill
½ teaspoon sea salt
1 egg*
2 tablespoons (30 g) plain whole-milk Greek yogurt*
½ cup (45 g) almond flour, plus more for dusting
Generous pat of butter or drizzle of extra-virgin olive
   oil, for cooking*
Lemon wedges, for garnish
*See Notes on page 41

To make the sauce: Whisk together the mustard and yogurt. Taste to see whether you'd like a sharper flavor (add more mustard) or a creamier texture (add more yogurt). Set aside.

   To make the cakes: In a large bowl, mix the crab, onion, Dijon, ground mustard, dill, salt, egg, and yogurt. Stir in the almond flour. The mixture should be dry enough to easily shape into patties, but not so dry that it falls apart. If it needs to be a little drier add another tablespoon or two of almond flour; if it seems too dry, add another tablespoon or two of Greek yogurt.

   Using a ¼-cup (60 ml) measure, scoop out 8 cakes and tightly pack the measuring cup. Tap out onto a cutting board or plate sprinkled with almond flour and then press down lightly to shape each cake into a rough 3-inch (7.5 cm) patty. Sprinkle again with almond flour.

   Heat a pat of butter or a drizzle of extra-virgin olive oil in a large skillet over medium heat for 1 minute. Add the crab cakes and sauté for 4 minutes, or until the bottoms are nicely browned. Carefully flip over to cook the other side. Place the cooked cakes on a wire rack.

   The cakes are tasty served warm or cold. Serve with the sauce and lemon wedges.

Yield: 8 cakes or 4 servings

■ (WHOLE-GRAIN) BREADED CHICKEN FINGERS WITH MUSTARD DIP

Soy-Free

These fingers can easily be made into a main salad dish by topping a fresh bowl of mixed greens with the breaded cooked chicken. The dip becomes a dressing, too—just thin with extra-virgin olive oil or water until you can drizzle it onto your salad. So simple! If you'd like a sweet-and-savory effect, whisk a splash of balsamic vinegar or honey into the dip/dressing before serving.

For the chicken fingers:
¾ cup (67 g) almond flour
¾ cup (105 g) finely ground cornmeal*
Sea salt and freshly ground black pepper, to taste
1 tablespoon (3 g) dried Italian herbs
Dash of cayenne pepper
1 egg*
1 pound (455 g) trimmed chicken breast, cut into 1-inch
   (2.5-cm) strips*
Generous pat of butter, for cooking*

For the dip:
¾ cup (180 g) plain whole-milk Greek yogurt*
1 tablespoon (15 g) or more Dijon mustard
Drizzle of honey if you'd like a honey-mustard dip,
   optional
See Notes on page 41

To make the chicken: Combine the almond flour, cornmeal, salt, pepper, herbs, and cayenne pepper in a flat-bottomed bowl. Crack the egg into another flat-bottomed bowl and lightly scramble with a fork. Dip each piece of chicken into the egg and then the breading mixture.

Heat a pat of butter in a large skillet over medium heat until the butter is completely melted. Add the chicken—cooking in batches, if necessary—and cook for 7 minutes, or until the thickest piece of chicken is opaque when cut through. Add more butter if the pan becomes dry. If the chicken is browning too quickly, reduce the heat to medium-low.

To make the dip: Stir together the yogurt and Dijon. Feel free to add more Dijon to taste—the whole-milk yogurt will be thick enough to still have a nice consistency for dipping. Add the honey and stir to combine. Refrigerate until chicken is ready.

Serve the chicken piping hot with the dipping sauce.

Yield: 4 servings

■ NOODLE-FREE MEXICAN LASAGNA

Nut-Free, Soy-Free, Egg-Free, Vegetarian

I first came across the zucchini-as-noodles concept within the context of raw cuisine, and I immediately wanted to transfer that idea into gluten-free dishes. After all, zucchini is easy to find and inexpensive. Let's take advantage of this versatile vegetable!

1 pound (455 g) sweet potatoes, peeled and sliced into
   1/4-inch-thick (6 mm) rounds
Extra-virgin olive oil, for cooking
1 small onion, chopped
1 cup (182 g) black beans, drained*
1 cup (227 g) frozen corn kernels, thawed*
1 teaspoon cumin

2 large or 3 small zucchini, cut into 1/4-inch-thick
   (6.4 mm) rounds or long slices
8 ounces (225 g) Monterey Jack, Colby, or mild
   Cheddar cheese, grated*
2 cups (454 g) fresh-style salsa, either store-bought
   or homemade
See Notes on page 41

Preheat the oven to 375°F (190°C, or gas mark 5). Fill a medium pot halfway with water and bring to a boil over high heat. Slide in the sweet potato slices and simmer uncovered for 5 minutes, reducing the heat to medium if the pot threatens to boil over. Drain well.

Heat a drizzle of oil in a medium skillet over medium heat. Add the onions and cook, stirring occasionally, for 5 minutes, or until the onions are soft and fragrant. Transfer to a large bowl and toss with the black beans, corn, and cumin.

Line the bottom of a glass 9 x 13-inch (23 x 33 cm) pan with half of the sweet potatoes, arranging them in a single layer. Add half of the zucchini in another layer. Spoon on the corn-and-bean mixture and sprinkle with half of the cheese. Dollop on half of the salsa and gently spread with the back of a spoon, trying not to dislodge the layers. Repeat with the remaining sweet potato and zucchini slices. Spread on the remaining salsa and top with the remaining cheese.

Bake for 25 minutes, or until the cheese is melted and bubbling. If you'd like, serve this with cooked brown rice and/or corn chips. Leftover lasagna can be refrigerated for up to 5 days. This lasagna is "juicy" because there aren't any noodles to soak up the liquid from the veggies and salsa, but that's okay—just treat the juice as a sauce!

Yield: one 9 x 13-inch (23 x 33 cm) pan

■ INDONESIAN CURRIED PEANUT PASTA

Dairy-Free, Egg-Free, Vegetarian

To make this pasta even more authentically Indonesian, use whole coconut milk instead of water to thin the sauce. Not only is coconut the go-to milk for most of Southeast Asia, but it also has a slightly sweet taste and a creamy texture that's perfect for sauces and soups. Plus, unlike dairy milk and cream, heating coconut milk won't cause it to curdle.

8 ounces (225 g) 100% buckwheat noodles (also called *soba*) or brown rice spaghetti
2 large carrots, peeled and cut into 1-inch (2.5 cm) matchsticks
8 ounces (225 g) snap peas
Drizzle of unrefined peanut oil or extra-virgin olive oil, for cooking
4 cloves garlic, chopped

1 tablespoon (15 ml) wheat-free tamari
¼ cup (65 g) natural peanut butter
Juice of 1 lime plus 1 lime, sliced into wedges, for garnish
2 teaspoons (4 g) curry powder
Handful of fresh cilantro leaves
Roasted peanuts, chopped, for garnish

Bring a large pot of water to a boil over high heat. Add the pasta and cook according to package directions. Five minutes before the pasta will be done, add the carrots and peas to the same pot and simmer. This saves you from having to cook the veggies separately. Drain the noodles and veggies and set aside.

While the noodles and veggies are cooking, drizzle the oil into a medium skillet and heat over medium-low heat for 1 minute. Add the garlic and sauté, stirring often, for 3 minutes, or until the garlic starts to soften. Stir in the tamari and peanut butter and cook the mixture for 1 minute. Add the lime juice and curry powder and cook for 1 or 2 more minutes. At this point, the mixture will be fairly thick and bubbly, so add 1 or 2 tablespoons (15 to 28 ml) of water to thin the sauce. You should wind up with a creamy, light-brown sauce. If you would like the sauce to be more salty, add another tablespoon of tamari.

Remove the pan from the heat and stir in the cilantro. Toss the sauce with the noodles and veggies and serve immediately, garnishing with a scattering of peanuts and wedges of lime.

Yield: 4 servings

■ BAKED MAC 'N' CHEESE STARRING BROWN RICE PASTA

Nut-Free, Soy-Free, Egg-Free, Vegetarian

When it comes to gluten-free pastas, we are living in a Golden Age! You used to be lucky if you could find refined white rice pasta, but nowadays you can easily find brown rice pasta, whole-corn pasta, quinoa pasta, even amaranth pasta. "Ancient grain" varieties of pastas blend a variety of nongluten grains. You might even stumble upon black bean noodles or mung bean fettucini. For this dish, I've used brown rice macaroni to most closely match traditional mac 'n' cheese, but feel free to use whatever whole-grain gluten-free pasta strikes your fancy.

8 ounces (225 g) brown rice elbow macaroni
3 tablespoons (42 g) butter*
3 tablespoons (30 g) brown rice flour
1 ¾ cups (415 ml) whole milk or half-and-half*
¼ cup (40 g) chopped sweet onions and/or chives

2 cups (240 g) grated strong-flavored cheese, such as
     Cheddar, Gruyère, or Asiago*
1 tablespoon (7 g) sweet paprika
Freshly ground black pepper, optional
See Notes on page 41

Preheat the oven to 350°F (180°C, or gas mark 4). Cook the macaroni according to package directions and drain well.

While the macaroni is cooking, heat the butter over medium-low heat until it melts. Whisk in the flour. Slowly pour in the milk, whisking constantly. The sauce will thicken as it cooks. As soon as you add the last trickle of milk, add the onions/chives. Cook, still whisking, for 1 or 2 more minutes, or until the sauce thickens. Whisk in the cheese in handfuls, reserving about ½ cup (60 g) to scatter on the top of the macaroni. Remove from the heat and whisk in the paprika and pepper.

Scoop the macaroni into a deep 1 ½-quart (1.4 L) glass baking pan or equivalent square baking dish and top with the remaining ½ cup (60 g) cheese. Bake for 30 minutes, or until the top is golden brown and bubbly.

Yield: 4 servings

■ GINGER, GARLIC & SESAME SOBA NOODLES

Nut-Free, Dairy-Free, Egg-Free

Yet another category of gluten-free whole-grain pasta is soba noodles. These traditional Japanese noodles are made from either 100 percent buckwheat or a blend of wheat and buckwheat. Obviously, in order to have a gluten-free dish, you need to find soba noodles that are 100 percent buckwheat. Made of roasted buckwheat, they'll be a dark brown color, and they'll have a pronounced nutty flavor that pairs well with strong flavors like the garlic, ginger, and sesame you'll be using in this dish. Most health-food stores have them, as do most Japanese grocers.

8 ounces (225 g) 100% buckwheat pasta (also called *soba*)
Generous drizzle of toasted sesame oil for noodle-tossing and cooking
1 yellow bell pepper, cored, seeded, and thinly sliced
8 ounces (225 g) button mushrooms, sliced
1 tablespoon (15 ml) wheat-free tamari
1 tablespoon (15 ml) rice vinegar
4 cloves garlic, chopped

6 green onions, green part only, chopped
1 small head bok choy, ends trimmed away, leaves roughly chopped
1 teaspoon ginger
2 tablespoons (16 g) toasted sesame seeds
½ pound (225 g) pork tenderloin, cut into ½-inch (1.3 cm) slices*
*See Notes on page 41

Prepare the soba noodles according to the package directions. Drain, rinse with warm water, and drain again. Place in a large bowl and gently toss with a slight drizzle of toasted sesame oil.

In a large skillet, heat a generous drizzle of the toasted sesame oil over medium heat for 1 minute. Add the peppers and mushrooms and cook, stirring occasionally, for 5 minutes, or until the mushrooms are soft and have shrunk to half their size. Add the remaining ingredients except for the pork and stir well to combine. Cook for 5 minutes, or until garlic is soft and fragrant.

Stir in the pork and cook for 4 to 5 minutes, or until the thickest piece of pork is opaque all the way through. Add the pork mixture to the noodles and toss gently to combine.

Serve promptly, seasoning with an additional drizzle of tamari and/or rice vinegar at the table if you like. Leftover noodles can be refrigerated for up to 3 days.

Yield: 4 servings

AFRICAN SWEET POTATO STEW

Soy-Free, Egg-Free

We think of peanuts and corn as the most American of foods, but they're equally embraced by African cooks (although more commonly in the form of whole or crushed peanuts rather than peanut butter). Both peanuts and corn are filling, inexpensive, and versatile ingredients that are especially ideal in stews, soups, and porridges.

Generous pat of butter or unrefined coconut oil or unrefined red palm oil, for cooking
1 small onion, chopped
1 large carrot, chopped
3 large collard leaves, chopped
3 cups (710 ml) chicken broth*
¾ cup (135 g) polenta*
1 small green banana, peeled and chopped (See Recipe Note)
1 tablespoon (7 g) sweet paprika

1 tablespoon (16 g) natural peanut butter
1 teaspoon ginger
¾ pound (340 g) sweet potatoes, peeled and cut into ½-inch (1.3 cm) cubes
½ pound (225 g) green beans, trimmed and cut into 1-inch (2.5 cm) lengths
*See Notes on page 41

Recipe Note

➤ Like many other tropical regions of the world, African cuisine uses unripe fruits as veggies: Green bananas, green papayas, and green mangoes are all welcome ingredients in savory dishes. Choose a still-green banana to include in this stew—it'll impart a hint of sweetness, plus its starchy nature will lend a creaminess to the stew.

Heat a dab of butter, coconut oil, or—if you're really adventurous and want to be authentic—red palm oil in a large pot until melted. Add the onions and carrots and cook, stirring occasionally, over medium-low heat for 5 minutes, or until the veggies are soft and the onions are fragrant. Stir in the chopped collards and cook for an additional 5 minutes.

Add the broth, polenta, banana, paprika, peanut butter, and ginger and bring the stew to a boil. Immediately reduce the heat to low and simmer, stirring often, for 10 minutes. To prevent the polenta from sticking to the bottom of the pot, when you stir it, be sure to scrape the bottom to bring up the polenta.

Increase the heat to medium and add the sweet potatoes. Simmer for 5 minutes, then stir in the green beans and simmer for a final 5 minutes. If the simmering action becomes a furious boil at any point, reduce the heat to low. Check to see if the potatoes and beans have reached their desired tenderness—if not, continue to simmer for another 5 minutes. Serve immediately. Leftover stew can be refrigerated for up to 5 days.

Yield: 4 servings

➤ Any color but red lentils
works for this dish. That's
because red lentils cook in
5 minutes flat, which means
that they would turn into
mush in this harira. But red
lentils are ideal when you
want fast-cooking lentils!

■ BREAK-THE-FAST CHICKPEA & LAMB HARIRA

Nut-Free, Soy-Free

North African cuisine has many glorious traditions, one of them being the use of what we consider "sweet" spices in savory settings. In this rich stew—commonly served during Ramadan to break the daily fast from sunrise to sundown—both cinnamon and ginger are featured alongside lamb, lentils, and chickpeas. Lemons are an important element here, too, which represents another pillar of North African (and Mediterranean and Middle Eastern) cuisine: the emphasis on citrus fruits, especially lemons, oranges, and limes. Moroccan preserved lemons, dried Persian limes, and a bevy of beverages made with orange blossom water are just a few examples of the citrus-enhanced dishes in some of the world's most prolific citrus-growing regions.

½ pound (225 g) ground lamb*
1 yellow onion, chopped
3 stalks celery, chopped
15 ounces (425 g) canned diced
    tomatoes
32 ounces (945 ml) chicken broth*
1 teaspoon turmeric
½ teaspoon cinnamon
½ teaspoon ginger

Dash of cayenne or crushed red
    pepper
¼ cup (48 g) dry lentils (See
    Recipe Note)
15 ounces (425 g) canned chickpeas*
Juice of ½ lemon
2 eggs*
Feta made with sheep or goat's
    milk for garnish*
See Notes on page 41

In a large soup pot, sauté the lamb, onion, and celery over medium heat for about 5 minutes, or until the lamb is cooked through. Stir in the tomatoes, broth, spices, lentils, and chickpeas. Reduce the heat to low and simmer for 25 minutes.

Increase the heat to medium and stir in the lemon juice. Crack the eggs into the soup and stir gently for 2 minutes to create delicate ribbons with the egg. Remove from the heat and serve promptly, garnishing with feta. Leftover harira can be refrigerated for up to 4 days. Like all tomato-based soups, harira gains flavor upon standing, so this makes a wonderful leftover meal!

Yield: 4 servings

■ SPICY SOUTHWESTERN CORN CHOWDER

Nut-Free, Soy-Free, Egg-Free

Ah, nothing says summer like fresh corn! But if you're pressed for time or don't have access to fresh corn, frozen organic sweet corn also works well. Just add the frozen kernels directly to the chowder and heat an extra minute or two to thaw them.

Kernels from 3 ears fresh corn or
    3 cups (681 g) frozen corn*
Extra-virgin olive oil, for cooking
1 medium onion, chopped
2 cups (475 ml) chicken broth*
15 ounces (425 g) canned diced
    tomatoes
15 ounces (425 g) canned black
    beans*
2 medium tomatoes, chopped

½ cup (86 g) raw quinoa, rinsed
1 tablespoon (3 g) dried oregano
Dash of cayenne or pinch of
    crushed red pepper
Pinch of chipotle powder, optional
½ cup (120 ml) half-and-half*
Fresh cilantro, chopped (See
    Recipe Note)
Avocado slices, for garnish
Tortilla chips, for serving
See Notes on page 41

> **Recipe Note**
> ....
> ➤ Cilantro tends to be a love-it-or-hate-it herb. If you're a big fan, use a generous handful of leaves in this chowder. If you're a little more hesitant, only include a few leaves, or simply garnish the individual portions with a sprig or two.

To prepare the fresh corn, bring a large soup pot half full of water to a boil over high heat. Ease the ears into it and simmer for 3 minutes. Promptly pull out the ears with tongs, rinse out the pot, and refill with cold water. Place the ears in the cold water and let cool while you prepare the rest of the ingredients. (If you don't promptly chill the ears, they'll continue to cook and will be too mushy.) Remove the ears and pat them dry. Hold the ears above a large bowl one at a time and use a sharp knife to cut the kernels into the bowl. Rinse out the large soup pot.

In the rinsed-out soup pot, heat a drizzle of oil and the onion over medium heat for about 5 minutes, or until the onions are fragrant and turning translucent. Stir in the broth, canned tomatoes, beans, fresh tomatoes, quinoa, and spices and simmer for 10 minutes, stirring occasionally and reducing the heat to medium-low if the simmer threatens to become a boil. Stir in the cooked corn, half-and-half, and cilantro and heat for another minute.

This soup can be served warm or cold. Either way, avocado and tortilla chips make nice accompaniments.

Yield: 4 servings

> ➤ Cut the cooking time for the wild rice from 50 minutes to about 15 minutes by letting the wild rice soak in the water for at least 6 hours before making the soup.

■ TOMATO-BASIL SOUP WITH WHITE BEANS & FETA

Nut-Free, Soy-Free, Egg-Free

When it comes to grains, wild rice ranks low on the glycemic index scale. That translates to less of a spike in blood sugar levels. In other words, when you make soup with wild rice instead of white rice, you'll enjoy more flavor as well as more nutrition. Plus, wild rice splits as it cooks, which makes for a pretty brown-and-white presentation.

1 cup (160 g) wild rice (See Recipe Note)
2 cups (475 ml) water
1 pound (455 g) ripe tomatoes
Extra-virgin olive oil, for cooking
1 medium yellow squash or zucchini, trimmed and sliced
1 small onion, chopped

32 ounces (945 ml) chicken broth*
15 ounces (425 g) canned Great Northern beans*
2 teaspoons (2.4 g) dried rosemary
Handful of fresh basil
Feta cheese, preferably made with sheep or goat's milk, for garnish*
*See Notes on page 41

Place the wild rice in a medium pot. Add the water and bring to a boil over high heat. Reduce the heat to low and simmer, covered, for 40 minutes, or until tender to the tooth. Drain if necessary.

Place the tomatoes in a large heatproof mixing bowl and completely cover with boiling water. Let sit for 5 minutes or until their skins have begun to split. As soon as you can comfortably handle the tomatoes, peel away the skins. Chop the tomatoes, catching and saving the runaway juice and seeds.

Heat a drizzle of oil in a soup pot over medium heat for 1 minute. Add the squash and onions and cook, stirring occasionally, for 5 minutes, or until the onions are soft and fragrant and the squash is lightly browned. Pour in the broth, undrained beans, and rosemary. Add the chopped tomatoes with their juice and seeds and bring the soup to a boil over medium-high heat. Reduce the heat to medium-low and simmer for 10 minutes to marry the flavors.

While the soup simmers, roll the basil leaves into tight cylinders and then cut ("chiffonade") them into thin slices. Crumble or chop the feta you'll be using as garnish.

Remove the soup from the heat and stir in the basil. Serve individual bowls of soup garnished with the feta. Leftover soup can be refrigerated for up to 3 days.

Yield: 4 servings

■ MIX AND MATCH PESTO

Dairy-Free, Soy-Free, Egg-Free, Vegetarian, 20 minutes

Classical traditions notwithstanding, pesto can be made in a variety of ways by pairing different fresh herbs and nuts/seeds with extra-virgin olive oil and garlic. As long as your fresh herb is not overly pungent and blends easily, it will make a great pesto. The same goes for seeds and nuts: Choose ones that aren't overpowering and will blend easily in your food processor. Experiment with mixing and matching the suggested herb and nut/seed combinations! Use the same proportions that are in this classic base recipe of basil and pine nuts.

4 cups (96 g) loosely packed basil
    leaves
½ cup (68 g) pine nuts

Pinch of sea salt
1 small clove garlic (See Recipe
    Note)
½ cup (120 ml) extra-virgin olive oil

Blend the basil, pine nuts, salt, and garlic in a food processor until you have fairly small pieces of nuts and basil, then drizzle in the oil while the processor is running, blending until smooth. If you want to be able to pour or easily toss the pesto, you might need to add a little more oil; if you want more of a paste, the ½ cup (120 ml) will work. Add more salt if desired and serve as you like—tossed with pasta or vegetables, on sandwiches, or mixed into a dip. If you serve it with pasta, reserve the cooking water. The pesto-coated pasta will be smoother if you toss the pasta with a little bit of the cooking water.

Leftover pesto can be placed in a small container, covered with a layer of oil, and refrigerated for up to 3 days. Alternatively, you can freeze it for up to a month.

Yield: 4 generous servings

Recipe Notes

➤ Here's a mix-and-match listing of different nuts and herbs you can use instead of just basil and pine nuts. Get creative!

Nuts and seeds: pistachios, sunflower seeds, pumpkin seeds, almonds, walnuts

Herbs: basil, lemon verbena, dill, oregano, cilantro, parsley

➤ Instead of using one raw garlic glove, sauté five cloves of minced garlic in extra-virgin olive oil over medium heat until soft and fragrant. Add to the food processor with the rest of the ingredients, making sure to include the cooking oil (and subtracting it from your total amount).

■ MEXICAN POZOLE WITH ALL THE TRIMMINGS

Nut-Free, Dairy-Free (omit the yogurt), Soy-Free, Egg-Free

Chayote is a member of the squash family: Think of it as the zucchini of the Latin world. You can often find chayote Stateside in Latin markets or in the "exotics" section of produce markets. Look for the light-green, fist-sized, teardrop-shaped squash with the puckered end. The flesh right underneath the skin is a little sticky, so when you peel the chayote, hold it underneath cool running water.

For the pozole:
Extra-virgin olive oil, for cooking
1 small onion, chopped
5 cloves garlic, chopped
2 cups (475 ml) chicken broth*
1 cup (235 ml) water
28 ounces (795 g) canned diced
   tomatoes
15 ounces (425 g) canned navy
   beans*
1 tablespoon (7.5 g) chili powder
1 chayote squash, peeled, spongy
   core removed, and cut into 1-inch
   (2.5 cm) cubes (See Recipe Note)
Sea salt, optional
15 ounces (425 g) canned yellow
   or white hominy, drained (See
   Recipe Note)

Optional toppings:
Cooked bacon, chopped*
   (See page 55)
Whole-milk plain Greek yogurt*
Chopped cilantro
Lime wedges
Thinly sliced cabbage
Chopped avocado
See Notes on page 41

Recipe Notes

➤ If you can't find chayote squash, substitute one medium sweet potato, peeled, and cut into 1-inch (2.5 cm) cubes.

➤ Look for canned hominy in the canned vegetables aisle or in the Mexican section of a well-stocked grocery store.

To make the pozole: Drizzle a splash of oil into a large soup pot. Add the onions and sauté over medium heat for 5 minutes, or until the onions are soft but not yet brown. Add the garlic, reduce the heat to medium-low, and cook for another 2 minutes, or until the garlic is fragrant and soft. Pour in the chicken broth, water, tomatoes, and beans. Stir in the chili powder and bring to a boil over medium-high heat.

Add the chayote, reduce the heat to a gentle simmer, and let the squash cook for 10 minutes. Poke a piece with the tip of a sharp knife to see if it has reached the desired tenderness. Add more chili powder and/or a dash of sea salt to taste.

To serve: Stir in the hominy, simmer for another minute, and serve. Garnish with any or all of the optional toppings. Leftover pozole can be refrigerated for up to 5 days. Like all tomato-based soups and sauces, the flavor deepens upon standing, so you may like it even better the next day!

Yield: 4 hearty servings

➤ If you would like a thicker, creamier soup, include the coconut milk. If you're not overly familiar with Vietnamese flavors, you might also wish to include the milk—it gives the soup a smoother, more muted flavor.

➤ If you can't find pomegranate molasses, tamarind paste has a similar sweet-tart flavor. Look for those two products in markets that stock Middle Eastern and/or Indian groceries.

■ VIETNAMESE-INSPIRED MUSHROOM, GREEN ONION & NOODLE SOUP

Dairy-Free, Egg-Free

Vietnamese food is all about balance: sweet and sour, earthy and crisp, salty and smooth. This soup contains all of these elements, from earthy mushrooms to sweet pomegranate molasses to salty, intensely savory fish sauce. The latter is what really evokes Vietnamese flavor. It has a strong taste, though, so if you're completely unfamiliar with Vietnamese and Thai dishes, start with ½ teaspoon. A little goes a long way! And don't be put off by the aroma of the fish sauce—it will blend into the soup to create a savory undertone, one that's not quite definable but would be missed if you took it away, much like the anchovies that go into Caesar salad dressing.

Unrefined coconut oil or extra-virgin olive oil, for cooking
8 ounces (225 g) button mushrooms, sliced
32 ounces (945 ml) chicken broth*
1 teaspoon fish sauce
2 teaspoons (10 ml) pomegranate molasses (See Recipe Note)
2 teaspoons (10 ml) wheat-free tamari
2 heads broccoli, florets only, cut into bite-size pieces
4 green onions, green part only, chopped

4 ounces (115 g) 100% buckwheat noodles (also called *soba*), broken into 2-inch (5 cm) lengths
4 ounces (115 g) water chestnuts, drained
Handful of bean sprouts, rinsed well
Juice of 1 lime
10 fresh mint leaves, minced
½ cup (120 ml) whole coconut milk, optional (See Recipe Note)
¼ to ½ pound (115 to 225 g) cooked chicken strips*, optional
*See Notes on page 41

Heat a dab of coconut oil in a large soup pot over medium-low heat until melted. Add the mushrooms and cook, stirring occasionally, for 5 minutes, or until mushrooms have shrunk to about half their original size. Pour in the broth, fish sauce, pomegranate molasses, and tamari.

Bring to a boil over medium-high heat and add the broccoli, green onions, and noodles. Reduce the heat to low and simmer for 5 minutes.

Stir in the water chestnuts, bean sprouts, lime juice, and mint and heat through for 1 minute. Stir in the coconut milk and chicken and remove from the heat. Serve promptly. Leftover soup can be refrigerated for up to 4 days.

Yield: 4 servings

■ ROASTED BUTTERNUT SQUASH SOUP

Nut-Free, Dairy-Free (omit the cheese), Soy-Free, Egg-Free

The winter squash family includes butternut, acorn, and the lesser-known buttercup. Butternut is usually the easiest one to find, but feel free to opt for any member of the winter squash family. The preparation is the same for whichever you choose: cut it in half, scoop out the seeds, and roast.

Handful of sun-dried tomatoes
1 medium butternut squash
Extra-virgin olive oil, for cooking
1 large Spanish onion, sliced
4 cloves garlic, chopped
32 ounces (945 ml) chicken broth*
1 tablespoon (1 g) dried sage leaves

Freshly ground black pepper
Sea salt, to taste
Minced green onion, for garnish
Grated Cheddar cheese, for garnish*, optional
Chopped cooked chicken, for garnish*, optional
See Notes on page 41

Place the sun-dried tomatoes in a bowl and cover with hot water. They can soften while you make the soup.

Preheat the oven to 375°F (190°C, or gas mark 5) and line a baking tray with foil or parchment paper. Trim both ends of the squash and cut it in half lengthwise. Scoop out the seeds and discard. Place the squash on the prepared tray and bake for 45 minutes or until the edges are browning and you can easily poke into the flesh with a knife. Remove from the oven and let cool. (This step can be done up to 3 days in advance.)

Heat a drizzle of oil in a large soup pot over medium heat. Add the onions and cook, stirring occasionally, for 8 minutes, or until the onions are fragrant and turning golden brown. Stir in the garlic and cook for another 2 minutes to soften the garlic. Pour in the broth and crumble the sage before adding it to the pot. Drain the tomatoes and stir them in along with a pinch of freshly ground pepper.

Reduce the heat to medium-low and let simmer for at least 10 minutes. While the soup simmers, scoop the cooled squash halves free of the skin. Stir the squash into the soup and heat through for another 2 minutes. Season to taste with sea salt. If you'd like to have supersmooth soup, let the soup cool to room temperature before running it through a blender. (Hot soup can be dangerously explosive when being blended!)

Serve immediately, garnished with the green onion, cheese, and/or chicken. Leftover soup can be refrigerated for up to 4 days.

Yield: 4 to 6 servings

■ CLASSIC (BUT BREADLESS) FRENCH ONION SOUP

Nut-Free, Soy-Free, Egg-Free

The whole secret to French onion soup is the slow-cooked onions. An hour may seem like a long time, but it's worth it—there's just no shortcut to achieving such a deep, caramelized flavor. And it doesn't take much effort to create such an impressive effect: Just stir the onions once in a while and let them do their slow-cooking thing. Oh, and don't skimp on the beef broth! No sense in ruining your gorgeous onions with a cheap broth filled with additives and chemicals. Opt for high-quality broth with an ingredient list you can easily under-stand. If possible, opt for one that's made with beef from grass-fed animals.

Butter or ghee, for cooking*
4 Spanish onions, sliced
32 ounces (945 ml) beef broth*
2 tablespoons (5.5 g) dried thyme
2 tablespoons (28 ml) sherry vinegar

Sea salt, to taste
Generous grinds of black pepper
4 whole-grain 100% corn tortillas*
1 cup (120 g) grated Gruyère cheese*
See Notes on page 41

Heat a hearty dab of butter in a large soup pot over medium-low heat until melted. Add the onions and cook for 15 minutes, stirring occasionally, or until the onions are softened. Continue to cook for another 45 minutes, or until the onions are very fragrant and have started to brown, stirring every 10 to 15 minutes so that the onions caramelize evenly.

Pour in the broth and stir in the thyme, vinegar, salt, and pepper. Bring the soup to a boil, then reduce the heat to low and simmer for 10 minutes. Turn on the oven broiler and get out 4 heatproof crocks that each hold at least 12 ounces (355 ml) of soup.

While the soup simmers, heat the tortillas by dry-toasting them for 2 to 3 minutes on each side in a large skillet over medium heat, until crisp and slightly browned. Remove from the heat.

Ladle the soup into the crocks and top each with a crisp tortilla and ¼ cup (30 g) of the cheese. Broil for 5 min-utes, or until the cheese is melted and starting to turn golden brown. Remove from the oven and let cool slightly. Leftover untopped soup can be refrigerated for up to 5 days.

Yield: 4 servings

■ SUMMERTIME GREENS & GARLIC SOUP

Nut-Free, Soy-Free, Egg-Free

In Spanish and Portuguese cookery, fideos are thin, thread-like noodles used in soups and stews. Some are long, but many are short, like punctuation marks for the dishes they grace with their delicate presence. It's easy enough to make your own fideos: Just break any thin gluten-free spaghetti into short pieces before adding them to the pot. I break mine over the pot so that any escaping pieces fall right into whatever I have simmering away.

1 small onion, chopped
Extra-virgin olive oil, for cooking
6 cloves garlic, chopped
32 ounces (945 ml) chicken broth*
Handful of green beans, trimmed
    and then chopped into 1-inch
    (2.5 cm) segments
1 bunch Swiss chard, chopped

Handful of brown rice spaghetti,
    broken into small pieces
Handful of fresh herbs, finely
    chopped (See Recipe Note)
Cherry tomatoes, halved, for garnish
Grated Parmesan, for garnish*
*See Notes on page 41

Cook the onions in a drizzle of oil in a large stockpot over medium heat for 5 minutes. Stir in the garlic and reduce the heat to medium-low. Cook, stirring often, for another 3 minutes, or just until the garlic is soft and fragrant. Pour in the broth and bring to a gentle boil. Add the beans and simmer for 3 minutes, reducing the heat if the boil becomes vigorous. Stir in the chard and noodles and continue to simmer for another 3 minutes, or until the noodles are cooked through.

Remove from the heat. Ladle the hot soup into individual bowls and garnish each serving with the herbs, tomatoes, and Parmesan. Leftover soup can be refrigerated for up to 4 days.

Yield: 4 servings

Recipe Note

➤ Basil, oregano, and/or marjoram work particularly well in this soup, although feel free to use whichever fresh herbs are your favorites. Another nice combination is dill and chives.

■ GAZPACHO WITH A TWIST

Nut-Free (omit almonds), Dairy-Free, Soy-Free, Egg-Free, Vegetarian, 20 minutes or less

This classic cold soup is perfect on a warm summer night when you don't want to cook: Combine all the ingredients, stir well, and enjoy. I've put a Mexican twist on the basic recipe by including cilantro and jalapeños, but if you'd prefer a more traditional approach, you can omit those.

½ English cucumber, ends trimmed but seeds and skin on, chopped
1 yellow bell pepper, cored, seeded, and chopped
¼ small onion, minced
1 clove garlic, minced
6 medium tomatoes, chopped
1 tablespoon (15 ml) red wine vinegar
Juice of ½ lemon

2 tablespoons (28 ml) extra-virgin olive oil
Sea salt and freshly ground pepper
11 ounces (325 ml) tomato juice
Handful of fresh cilantro, minced
1 tablespoon (9 g) minced jarred jalapeños, optional
Handful of toasted almonds, optional (See sidebar)

Combine the cucumber, bell pepper, onion, garlic, tomatoes, vinegar, lemon juice, and olive oil in a large bowl and toss well. Add a dash of sea salt and a few grinds of fresh peppercorns and toss again. Pour in the tomato juice and add the cilantro and jalapeños. Toss well again. By now, all the tossing should have encouraged the tomatoes to begin to break down and release their juices. If the gazpacho is still too thick for your taste, add more tomato juice or some water. If you'd like it to be a little more tart, add more lemon juice.

Serve individual portions of gazpacho topped with the toasted almonds.

Yield: about 4 cups

Chapter 10 | Appetizers & Snacks: Little Meals & Party Plates

Snack food doesn't have to be junk food. From dips to chips, it's easy to make your own nutritious nibbles. (Bet you can't eat just one kale chip!) Time to make your own staples—DIY sodas, gourmet hot chocolates, and savory crackers are just a recipe away.

■ THE ULTIMATE WHOLE-GRAIN SNACK: HOMEMADE POPCORN

Soy-Free, Egg-Free, Vegetarian, 20 minutes or less

Just ½ cup (105 g) raw kernels yields 16 cups of popcorn—about enough for 4 people. Any extra toppings can be saved and used to season a variety of dishes, from sautéed chicken to poached fish.

For Mesquite BBQ Popcorn:
¼ cup (30 g) chili powder
1 tablespoon (7 g) mesquite powder

For Cayenne Parmesan Popcorn:
½ cup (50 g) grated Parmesan*
Pinch of cayenne pepper

For Berbere-Dusted Popcorn:
¼ cup (28 g) sweet paprika
2 teaspoons (12 g) sea salt
1 teaspoon ginger
⅛ teaspoon cardamom
½ teaspoon nutmeg
⅛ teaspoon ground cloves
¼ teaspoon cinnamon
¼ teaspoon allspice
Pinch of cayenne pepper
½ teaspoon ground fenugreek (See Recipe Note)

For the popcorn:
½ cup (105 g) popcorn kernels*
1 tablespoon (14 g) ghee, butter*, or coconut oil
   (if using stove top method)
Melted butter or extra-virgin olive oil, to taste
   (See Recipe Note)
Fine sea salt, to taste
*See Notes on page 41

To make the seasoning mix: Combine the chosen blend of ingredients in a small bowl. Set aside.

If you have a popcorn maker: Pop the corn according to the manufacturer's instructions, then pour into a large mixing bowl. Toss well with the melted butter or olive oil and seasoning. Add fine sea salt to taste.

If you don't have a popcorn maker: In a pot that's deep but not too heavy—you'll be shaking it constantly—melt 1 tablespoon (14 g) of ghee, butter, or coconut oil over medium-high heat. Add the popcorn kernels to the pot. Cover the pot with a tight-fitting lid.

With an oven mitt on one hand, hold the lid down firmly. With the unmitted hand, start shaking the pot. You can rest for a few seconds now and again, but if you don't shake the pot almost constantly, you'll burn the popcorn. After a minute or so, you'll hear rapid popping. Keep shaking. When the popping slows to a crawl, pour the popcorn out of the pot and into a large bowl. Toss the popcorn with melted butter or oil and your chosen seasonings and add fine sea salt to taste. Serve immediately.

Recipe Notes
....
➤ Instead of melted butter or olive oil, try using another unrefined oil for serving, such as walnut or hazelnut oil.
➤ Look for fenugreek in well-stocked spice stores such as Penzey's.

➤ Basil, dill, and oregano are particularly suitable herbs for these melts, but feel free to use whichever herbs are your favorites.

➤ If you don't have a grill, you can sauté the polenta slices over medium-high heat on the stove until their exteriors are firm but their interiors still feel a little soft. Top them and finish them under your oven broiler.

■ GRILLED POLENTA MELTS

Nut-Free, Soy-Free, Egg-Free, Vegetarian, 20 minutes or less

Polenta dates back to the Roman empire—soldiers and centurions alike carried polenta as part of their daily rations. It's essentially cornmeal cooked into porridge and then squeezed into a log shape. Polenta's mild flavor makes it a willing partner for the savory cheese, fresh herbs, and juicy tomatoes featured in this recipe.

One 1-pound (455 g) log of polenta*
Extra-virgin olive oil
Sea salt and freshly ground pepper
Aged savory cheese, such as Gouda, Asiago, or Cheddar, cut into thin slices*

Fresh herb of your choice, roughly chopped (See Recipe Note)
2 large tomatoes, thinly sliced
See Notes on page 41

Preheat the grill to high.

Cut the polenta into ¾-inch (2 cm) slices and place in a large bowl. Drizzle generously with oil and sprinkle with sea salt and freshly ground pepper. Toss gently with your hands until the polenta slices are well coated with oil. If they aren't glossy with oil, they'll stick to the grill!

Arrange the polenta slices evenly over the lower rack of the grill. Medium heat is ideal if you're using a gas-powered/adjustable grill. Depending on how hot the grill is, let slices cook for 5 to 10 minutes before gently flipping over. Repeat with the second side. The polenta should be crisp on the exterior but not charred; when you push on it gently with tongs, the interior should still feel soft. As it cooks, the polenta will also shrink into tighter disks.

Using tongs, temporarily place the polenta slices on a tray. Top each with a slice of cheese, a sprinkling of herbs, and a tomato slice. Carefully transfer the polenta to the upper rack of the grill (or the coolest spot if you're using a single-rack grill) and let cook for another 1 to 2 minutes to melt the cheese. Serve immediately.

Yield: 4 servings.

HUMMUS THREE WAYS: RED PEPPER, CILANTRO & ROASTED EGGPLANT

Nut-Free, Dairy-Free, Soy-Free, Egg-Free, Vegetarian, 20 minutes or less

Sautéing the garlic with a generous drizzle of extra-virgin olive oil creates a smoother, more balanced hummus rather than one that's garlic-forward. If you'd rather have a more garlicky hummus, swap the sautéed garlic for 1 small clove of raw garlic.

Variations:

1 roasted red pepper, cored, seeded, and chopped
1 bunch cilantro, leaves only
1 small roasted or sautéed eggplant, skin on, mashed

1 batch classic hummus (see Collard-Wrapped Tuna & Hummus Rolls recipe on page 59)

To make one of the variations, blend the roasted pepper, cilantro, or eggplant into a batch of classic hummus. Leftover hummus can be refrigerated for up to 5 days.

Yield: about 2 cups (492 g); about 3 cups (738 g) for the Roasted Eggplant Hummus

MEDITERRANEAN EGGPLANT CAPONATA

Nut-Free, Soy-Free, Egg-Free, Vegetarian

When it comes to eggplants, the fewer seeds they contain, the sweeter they'll taste. Less-seedy eggplants are typically younger eggplants, so no matter the variety of eggplant—baby, Italian, striped—look for eggplants with smooth, taut, glossy skin. Any blemishes or puckering indicate an eggplant is past its prime.

Extra-virgin olive oil, for cooking
1 small onion, chopped
1 red pepper, cored, seeded, and chopped
2 celery stalks, chopped
2 baby eggplants or 1 medium eggplant, ends trimmed but skin on, chopped
½ teaspoon cumin
½ teaspoon coriander

½ teaspoon sweet paprika
2 tablespoons (28 ml) maple syrup
3 tablespoons (45 ml) red wine vinegar
15 ounces (425 g) canned diced tomatoes
Chopped cilantro, for garnish
Feta made with goat and/or sheep's milk, for garnish*
See Notes on page 41

Heat a drizzle of oil in a large skillet over medium heat for a minute before adding the onion, pepper, and celery. Sauté for 5 minutes, or until the onion is soft and fragrant. Reduce the heat to medium-low and stir in the eggplant and spices.

Sauté for an additional 5 minutes, or until the eggplant is soft. Add the maple syrup, vinegar, and tomatoes, reduce heat to low, and let simmer for 20 minutes.

Serve as a chunky dip garnished with cilantro and feta, or use as a sauce for anything from grilled chicken to brown rice. The caponata can be refrigerated for up to 4 days or frozen for up to 3 months.

Yield: about 4 cups (800 g)

■ WHITE BEAN & ARTICHOKE DIP

Nut-Free, Soy-Free, Egg-Free, Vegetarian, 20 minutes or less

Fresh artichokes are one of spring's most impressive vegetables, but cutting away the outer layers to reveal the heart can be time-consuming. But don't despair—frozen hearts are a gift from the culinary gods.

Extra-virgin olive oil, for cooking
1 small onion, chopped
8 ounces (225 g) frozen artichoke hearts, thawed
15 ounces (425 g) canned Great Northern beans*
½ cup (115 g) plain whole-milk Greek yogurt*

¾ cup (75 g) grated Parmesan*
1 tablespoon (3 g) dried oregano
½ teaspoon sea salt
See Notes on page 41

Place a drizzle of oil in a medium skillet over medium heat. Add the onions and cook, stirring occasionally, for 7 minutes or until the onions are soft and translucent. Place all the ingredients in a food processor and blend until smooth. Serve the dip with whole-grain pretzel sticks or crunchy veggies such as carrots or celery.

Yield: about 3 ½ cups (900 g)

■ DAL (INDIAN LENTIL DIP)

Nut-Free, Soy-Free, Egg-Free, Vegetarian

Pappadums look like tortillas, but they're wafer-thin crispy rounds made of chickpea, lentil, rice, and/or potato flour. Cook them over medium heat in a generous dab of ghee or butter until each side is puffed and crispy.

2 cups (475 ml) water
⅔ cup (129 g) brown lentils
Butter or ghee, for cooking*
1 yellow bell pepper, cored, seeded, and chopped
1 small onion, chopped
2 large tomatoes, chopped
1 teaspoon ground ginger

2 teaspoons (4 g) coriander
2 teaspoons (5 g) cumin
2 teaspoons (7.5 g) mustard seeds
2 teaspoons (10 ml) pomegranate molasses, optional
½ teaspoon sea salt
See Notes on page 41

Bring the water to a boil in a medium pot over medium-high heat. Add the lentils, reduce the heat, and simmer for 15 to 20 minutes, or until the lentils have reached the desired tenderness. Drain.

Melt a dab of ghee or butter in a large skillet over medium heat. Add the pepper and onion and cook for 5 minutes, stirring occasionally, or until the onions are soft and fragrant. Add the remaining ingredients, reduce the heat to medium-low, and cook for 10 minutes, or until the tomatoes are very soft. If the veggies start to bubble furiously, reduce the heat to low. Stir in the cooked and drained lentils. If you'd like a smooth dal, let the lentil mixture cool slightly and then run it through a food processor until smooth.

Should you be lucky enough to stumble upon pappadums in an Indian grocery store, they would be lovely served with the dal. Alternatively, whole-grain gluten-free crackers, carrot and celery sticks, and/or tortilla chips are great dippee candidates.

Yield: about 3 cups (750 g)

◀ SESAME & SUNFLOWER KALE CHIPS

Nut-Free, Dairy-Free, Egg-Free, Vegetarian

Nutritional yeast is a nonleavening yeast used as a savory flavoring, most notably as a cheese stand-in for vegans. Look for it in health-food stores.

1 bunch kale, rinsed
¼ cup (36 g) sunflower seeds, raw or toasted
¼ cup (36 g) sesame seeds, raw or toasted

1 tablespoon (3 g) dried Italian herbs
1 tablespoon (5 g) nutritional yeast
1 tablespoon (15 ml) wheat-free tamari

Preheat the oven to 325°F (170°C, or gas mark 3) and cover 2 baking sheets with parchment paper.

Whack the kale dry against the edge of the sink, rip the tough ribs away from each leaf, and discard the ribs. Tear the leaves into small pieces and place in a large bowl.

Using a coffee/spice grinder, grind the seeds with the Italian herbs. Add the nutritional yeast and grind again. Drizzle the kale lightly with tamari, add the seasoning mix, and use your hands to scrunch the leaves and the seasoning together to get the seasoning to stick. The goal is to have just enough tamari to make the leaves a little bit wet so that the seeds will stick. Too wet, and the leaves will never get crispy in the oven.

Spread the chips out on baking sheets so that none overlap and bake for 20 minutes, or until the chips are crispy.

Yield: 2 to 4 servings

■ CRISPY PAN-FRIED CHICKPEAS

Nut-Free, Dairy-Free, Soy-Free, Egg-Free, Vegetarian, 20 minutes or less

These crispy 'peas make great dinner party appetizers because you can use whatever spice blend you like to flavor them. Indian-themed dinner? Opt for curry powder instead of berbere. A Mexican meal? Use chili powder.

1 to 2 tablespoons (15 to 28 ml) extra-virgin olive oil
15 ounces (425 g) canned chickpeas, drained well*

1 tablespoon (7 g) berbere (see page 113), chili powder, or your favorite spice mix
Sea salt, optional
*See Notes on page 41

Drizzle 1 tablespoon (15 ml) of the oil into a medium nonstick skillet. You want a skillet just big enough to accommodate all of the chickpeas in one layer. There should be enough oil to cover the bottom of the skillet.

Heat the oil for a minute over medium heat, then add the drained chickpeas. Sauté for 15 to 20 minutes, or until the chickpeas turn golden brown (several will crack and split slightly), shaking the pan occasionally to roll the chickpeas around. While they're cooking, lay several pieces of paper toweling on a large plate.

Roll the cooked chickpeas onto the paper towels and let drain for 1 minute. Pour them into a large bowl and toss them with the spices. Taste and toss in more spice if you'd like, plus a pinch of sea salt.

These miniature spicy appetizers are best served hot, but they're tasty at room temperature, too. If you have any left over, refrigerate for up to 4 days alone, as salad toppers, or tossed with other veggies.

Yield: about 1 ½ cups (270 g)

■ AMARANTH PIZZA MUFFINS
Nut-Free, Soy-Free

Like quinoa, amaranth is a complete protein. Wheat isn't. That means these amaranth- and quinoa-based pizza muffins are much more filling and nutritious than a typical slice of pizza could ever be. Combined with savory chickpea flour, herbs, and typical "pizza" ingredients like pepperoni and mozzarella, these muffins make a great lunch.

Extra-virgin olive oil, for cooking, plus ¼ cup (60 ml)
½ yellow bell pepper, flesh only, minced
½ small onion, minced
1 cup (160 g) amaranth flour
½ cup (70 g) chickpea flour
½ cup (56 g) quinoa flour
2 teaspoons (9 g) baking powder
½ teaspoon sea salt

¼ cup (15 g) chopped sun-dried tomatoes
1 tablespoon (3 g) dried Italian herbs
1 teaspoon oregano
½ cup (65 g) chopped pepperoni or salami*
3 eggs*
½ cup (120 ml) whole milk*
1 cup (150 g) grated mozzarella cheese*
See Notes on page 41

Preheat the oven to 350°F (180°C, or gas mark 4) and line a muffin tin with 12 parchment cups.

Heat a drizzle of oil in a medium skillet over medium-low heat. Add the bell pepper and onion and cook, stirring often, for 8 minutes, or until the veggies are very soft. Remove from the heat.

While the veggies cook, place the flours, baking powder, salt, sun-dried tomatoes, and herbs in a large bowl and whisk to combine. In another bowl, whisk together the pepperoni, eggs, milk, mozzarella, and ¼ cup (60 ml) oil. Whisk in the cooked veggies.

Stir the wet ingredients into the dry until well blended. Scoop the batter into the waiting muffin tins and bake for 22 minutes, or until a toothpick inserted into the center muffin comes out clean and warm. Muffins must be refrigerated! They can be kept for up to 4 days.

Yield: 12 muffins

■ SAVORY SALSA-AND-BLACK-BEAN CORNBREAD

Nut-Free, Soy-Free, Vegetarian

When it comes to grains, one of the least-starchy grains is buckwheat. It's a fantastic grain for diabetics, prediabetics, and anyone who does not want to become diabetic. Buckwheat is my number one grain choice for baked goods. Unfortunately, though, most buckwheat flour is milled from roasted buckwheat, which has a strong flavor that sometimes interferes with baked goods. I prefer the milder flavor of raw buckwheat . . . which is nearly impossible to find as preground flour. Enter high-speed processors and flour mills! They make grinding your own flour as easy as flipping a switch and waiting 20 seconds. If you can't find/make raw buckwheat flour, brown rice and sorghum flours are both good substitutes, albeit more starchy. If you're an avid baker, it's worth investing in a high-speed processor or flour mill.

1 ¼ cups (210 g) cornmeal, preferably stone-ground*
¾ cup (90 g) raw buckwheat flour or brown rice flour
1 tablespoon (14 g) baking powder*
½ teaspoon sea salt
1 cup (227 g) fresh-style salsa, either homemade or store-bought

2 eggs*
1 cup (182 g) canned black beans, drained*
½ cup (120 ml) whole milk*
1 cup (115 g) shredded Monterey Jack or mozzarella cheese*
*See Notes on page 41

Preheat the oven to 425°F (220°C, or gas mark 7) and thoroughly grease a glass 8 x 8-inch (20 x 20 cm) pan.

In a large bowl, whisk together the cornmeal, buckwheat flour, baking powder, and salt. In a smaller bowl, whisk together the remaining ingredients. Stir the wet ingredients into the dry until well blended.

Pour into the pan and bake for 25 to 28 minutes, or until a toothpick inserted into the center comes out clean and warm.

Yield: one 8 x 8-inch (20 x 20 cm) pan

◀ QUINOA-STUFFED BAKED POTATOES WITH ALL THE FIXINGS

Nut-Free, Soy-Free, Egg-Free

Who doesn't like a stuffed baked potato? Especially when the potato is stuffed with protein-rich, satisfying quinoa.

2 Idaho baking potatoes
⅔ cup (160 ml) water
⅓ cup (58 g) raw quinoa, rinsed
½ cup (120 g) plain whole-milk Greek yogurt*
2 green onions, green part only, minced

4 strips cooked bacon, chopped* (see page 55)
1 cup (115 g) freshly shredded Cheddar cheese*
See Notes on page 41

Preheat the oven to 375°F (190°C, or gas mark 5). Pierce each potato in several places with a fork. Place directly on the rack and bake for 1 hour or until easily pierced with a fork. Cool on a wire rack. Keep the oven on.

Bring the water to a boil in a medium pot over medium-high heat. Add quinoa. Simmer over medium-low heat for 10 to 15 minutes, or until you see cute quinoa "tails" and they've absorbed all of the water. Remove from the heat.

When you can comfortably handle them, cut each potato in half lengthwise. Carefully scoop out the interiors of the potatoes, leaving the skins behind. Place half of the baked potato flesh in a large bowl and reserve the other half for another use. Mash the potatoes with the Greek yogurt. Stir in the cooked quinoa, green onions, and bacon.

Fill each potato half with the quinoa mixture, then top each with ¼ cup (28 g) of the Cheddar. Place on a foil-lined baking tray or pan and bake for 25 minutes, or until the cheese is melted and bubbling.

Yield: 4 stuffed potatoes

■ UMAMI BLISS: MUSHROOM TAPENADE

Nut-Free, Dairy-Free, Soy-Free, Egg-Free, Vegetarian, 20 minutes or less

Not only is this ultra-savory tapenade ideal as a dip, but it also makes a great base for sauces, marinades, and dressings. Or freeze it in ice cube trays for easy access in case you'd like to have the tapenade on hand as an instant soup seasoning.

Extra-virgin olive oil, for cooking
8 ounces (225 g) mushrooms, sliced
1 small onion, chopped
6 cloves garlic, chopped

20 pitted black kalamata olives
15 ounces (425 g) canned diced tomatoes
1 tablespoon (3 g) dried Italian herbs

Place a drizzle of oil in a large skillet over medium heat. Add the mushrooms and onions and sauté for 8 minutes. Stir in the garlic and olives and cook for 3 minutes. Add the tomatoes and herbs and let simmer for at least 10 minutes, reducing heat to medium-low if the tapenade is bubbling too furiously.

Let cool, then purée the finished tapenade in a food processor until smooth.

Yield: about 2 cups (450 g)

◀ SAVORY BRUSSELS SPROUT "TRUFFLES"

Nut-Free, Soy-Free, Egg-Free, Vegetarian, 20 minutes or less

Eight minutes is the sweet spot when cooking brussels sprouts. If you hit 10 minutes, the sulfur compounds in your sprouts will start to break down and release their not-so-nice aroma (a.k.a. the dreaded "cabbage smell"). Don't cook your sprouts longer than 8 minutes!

24 bite-size brussels sprouts
Grated Parmesan, to taste*

Several grinds of black pepper
See Notes on page 41

Trim away the bottoms of the sprouts. If there are any discolored outer leaves, pull those off and discard. Rinse the sprouts well. Fill a medium pot halfway with water and bring to a boil over high heat. Add the sprouts, reduce the heat to medium, and simmer for 8 minutes. Drain immediately.

Sprinkle the cheese and pepper onto a large plate. Poke a toothpick into the base of each sprout and roll in the Parmesan until each sprout is a cheese-covered "truffle." Serve within an hour of making them.

Yield: 24 pieces

■ BAKED MOCHI BRUSCHETTA

Dairy-Free, Soy-Free, Egg-Free, Vegetarian, 20 minutes or less

Look for Grainaissance brand baked mochi in health-food stores. (Often, you'll find it in the frozen section.) Store it in the freezer until a day or two before you're going to use it, then leave it in the refrigerator to thaw. Otherwise, it's literally too hard to cut into cubes.

12 ½ ounce (354 g) block plain brown rice mochi,
   at room temperature
4 medium ripe and juicy tomatoes, chopped
2 green onions, green part only, minced
1 medium zucchini, ends trimmed, chopped

2 tomatillos, husks removed, chopped
¼ cup (35 g) pine nuts
1 tablespoon (15 ml) balsamic vinegar
2 tablespoons (28 ml) extra-virgin olive oil
Sea salt and freshly ground black pepper, to taste

Preheat the oven to 450°F (230°C, or gas mark 8). Cut the mochi into 1-inch (2.5 cm) squares and place on an uncovered and ungreased baking sheet, spacing them evenly apart. Bake for 10 to 12 minutes. You'll see the squares puff up and turn golden brown.

While the mochi bakes, make the bruschetta sauce by combining all the remaining ingredients in a large bowl. Toss well to combine. Serve the sauce with the puffy mochi squares. The squares can be pulled apart, revealing their hollow and very fillable interiors. It's fun to spoon a little bit of the sauce into each half.

Yield: 4 servings, about 2 cups (454 g) sauce

➤ Mint is also a main ingredient in Greek tzatziki, a yogurt-based condiment flavored with mint, garlic, cucumbers, and often lemon juice. A dollop of plain whole-milk Greek yogurt would be a nice accompaniment to these meatballs, or make a quick version of tzatziki by combining yogurt with minced seedless cucumber, a clove of minced garlic, some chopped fresh mint, and a squeeze of lemon juice.

■ MOROCCAN ALMOND & LAMB MEATBALLS

Dairy-Free, Soy-Free

Along with "sweet" spices like cinnamon and ginger, North African (and Mediterranean and Middle Eastern) cuisines also feature mint as a main flavor in savory dishes. No, it's not just for mojitos and candy canes! Mint pairs beautifully with the assertive flavor of lamb and goat, meats that are far more common than beef in Morocco and its surrounding regions.

1 pound (455 g) ground lamb, or ½ pound (225 g) ground beef plus ½ pound (225 g) ground lamb*
1 tablespoon (10 g) minced red onion
2 cloves garlic, minced
Grated zest of 1 orange
2 teaspoons (5 g) cumin
2 teaspoons (4 g) coriander

1 tablespoon (1.5 g) dried mint (See Recipe Note)
1 teaspoon sea salt
1 egg*
½ cup (45 g) almond flour, or more as needed
Drizzle of extra-virgin olive oil, for cooking, if needed
*See Notes on page 41

Mix the lamb with the onion, garlic, orange zest, spices, salt, and egg. Add enough almond flour to make a mixture that is dry enough to easily roll into 1-inch (2.5 cm) balls. If you overshoot on the dryness, add another egg and gradually add in more almond flour until you hit the right consistency.

Sauté the balls over medium heat for 4 minutes, or until all "sides" are nicely browned, shaking the pan often to make sure the meatballs cook evenly. (When you think they're done, remove one and cut it in half to see whether it's cooked through.) If the meatballs stick to the pan while cooking, add a drizzle of extra-virgin olive oil and carefully move them around to unstick them.

Serve on a large plate with a toothpick inserted into each meatball and tzatziki sauce on the side (see Recipe Note).

Yield: about 50 meatballs

■ THAI PORK & GINGER MEATBALLS

Dairy-Free, Soy-Free (use fish sauce)

Most meatballs contain tasteless bread crumbs as binders. Not these! For this dish, you'll be taking advantage of your coffee/spice grinder to make raw cashew and almond flours. The creamy flavor of cashews and the nutty savoriness of the almonds complements the flavorful cilantro, fish sauce, and garlic.

1 pound (455 g) ground pork*
1 egg*
¼ cup (4 g) chopped cilantro
Juice of ½ lime
2 cloves garlic, minced
3 green onions, green part only, minced
¼ teaspoon cayenne
1 teaspoon fish sauce or gluten-free tamari
2 teaspoons (3.6 g) ground ginger

2 teaspoons (28 ml) pomegranate molasses or tamarind paste (See Recipe Note)
1 cup (140 g) raw cashew flour (See Recipe Note)
½ cup (45 g) almond flour (See Recipe Note)
Extra-virgin olive oil, for cooking
*See Notes on page 41

Place all the ingredients in a large bowl and mix with your hands. Shape into 1-inch (2.5 cm) balls, placing each on a large plate as you go. Note that the meatballs will be more sticky and loose compared to conventional meatballs.

Heat a drizzle of oil in a large nonstick skillet over medium heat for 1 minute, then add the first batch of meatballs. Don't overcrowd the pan! You'll need room to maneuver a spatula, so you'll probably need to cook the meatballs in 3 batches.

Cook the meatballs undisturbed for 5 minutes, then gently flip each one over and cook for another 5 minutes. If the meatballs are browning too fast, reduce the heat to medium-low. Gently shake the pan and cook for a final 2 minutes, or until the thickest meatball is opaque throughout when cut in half.

Place the cooked meatballs on a rack to drain while you make the second and third batches. The successive batches will only need 4 minutes of cooking time per "side" because the skillet will be hotter. Finish each batch by cooking them for 2 minutes. If the meatballs seem to be browning too fast, reduce the heat slightly.

Serve the meatballs on toothpicks as appetizers or tossed with 100 percent buckwheat soba noodles and sautéed veggies as a complete meal. Or try serving the meatballs with PB, Soy & Ginger Dipping Sauce (page 129).

Yield: about 50 meatballs

■ SPICY CHILI SAUCE

Nut-Free, Dairy-Free, Egg-Free, Vegetarian

This sauce is fabulous on hot dogs, hamburgers, or anything that you'd normally slather with ketchup. It can be refrigerated for up to two weeks in a jar for handy access.

Extra-virgin olive oil, for cooking
1 small onion, diced
3 cloves garlic, chopped
1 cup (245 g) tomato sauce
1 teaspoon ground mustard or mustard seeds
½ teaspoon allspice

1 teaspoon maple syrup
1 tablespoon (15 ml) red wine vinegar
1 tablespoon (15 ml) wheat-free tamari
Pinch of sea salt and freshly ground black pepper
Crushed red pepper, optional

Place a drizzle of oil in a medium pot over medium heat. Add the onion and sauté for 5 minutes, or until the onion is soft. Add the garlic and cook 2 or 3 minutes, or until the garlic is fragrant and just starting to turn light brown. Add the remaining ingredients, stir to combine, and reduce the heat to low. Let simmer for about 20 minutes to allow the flavors to marry and the sauce to thicken. Refrigerate for up to 2 weeks.

Yield: about 1 cup (275 g)

■ PB, SOY & GINGER DIPPING SAUCE

Dairy-Free, Egg-Free, Vegetarian, 20 minutes or less

This flavorful sauce is perfect to serve with chicken on skewers as a dip, or toss it with cooked noodles and sautéed veggies. Beef pairs surprisingly well with peanut butter–based sauces, too.

Extra-virgin olive, for cooking
8 cloves garlic, chopped
2 tablespoons (28 ml) wheat-free tamari
½ cup (130 g) natural peanut butter (See Recipe Note)
Pinch of cayenne pepper or crushed red pepper flakes

Juice of 1 lime
2 teaspoons (3.6 g) ground ginger
2 to 3 tablespoons (28 to 45 ml) water
Handful of fresh cilantro leaves, minced

Place a drizzle of oil in a medium skillet over medium-low heat. Add the garlic and sauté for 3 minutes, or until the garlic is starting to soften. Stir in the tamari, peanut butter, and cayenne and let the mixture cook for 1 minute. Add the lime juice and ginger and cook for 1 or 2 more minutes.

At this point, the mixture will be fairly thick and bubbly, so add 2 tablespoons (28 ml) of the water to thin the sauce. Add the remaining 1 tablespoon (15 ml) of water if needed. You'll wind up with a creamy, light brown sauce. Remove pan from heat and stir in the cilantro. Refrigerate for up to 4 days.

Yield: about ¾ cup (336 g)

> **Recipe Note**
> ....
> ➤ If you use salted peanut butter, you may wish to lessen the amount of wheat-free tamari or use low-sodium wheat-free tamari.

ROASTED PEPPERS

Place a sheet of aluminum foil on the bottommost rack of your oven to catch any drips coming from the pepper.

Preheat the oven to 425°F (220°C, or gas mark 7). Place the peppers directly on the middle rack, centering them over the foil. Roast for 10 to 15 minutes, or until all sides are blackened and blistering. *Note:* The larger the pepper, the longer the roasting will take, so it's best to choose peppers of a similar size so they roast at the same rate.

Slip the roasted peppers into a plastic bag. Seal the bag and let the peppers sit until they're cool enough to handle. Work with the peppers over a cutting board—water will leak out of the peppers as you handle them. Pull away the seeds and stem and discard. Either chop the pepper to use in salads or blend it in a food processor to incorporate the roasted pepper into sauces, soups, dips, hummus, you name it! Refrigerate for up to 5 days.

■ CHUNKY ROASTED RED PEPPER & OLIVE SAUCE

Nut-Free, Dairy-Free, Soy-Free, Egg-Free, Vegetarian, 20 minutes or less

Roasting peppers is much easier than you think, but if you don't have time to roast your own, opt for jarred roasted peppers. Look for them near the pickles and jarred olives, and look for peppers that are in water—not oil—with no sugar added. Once opened, use the peppers within a week.

Extra-virgin olive oil, for cooking
½ small onion, chopped
4 ounces (115 g) button or baby bella mushrooms, quartered
½ medium eggplant, ends trimmed, skin on, chopped
4 cloves garlic, chopped

1 tablespoon (15 ml) water
2 ounces (55 g) pitted black kalamata olives, minced
1 teaspoon rosemary or dried Italian seasoning
1 red bell pepper, roasted, flesh chopped (see sidebar)

Place a drizzle of oil in a large skillet over medium heat. Add the onions and cook the 5 minutes, or until the onions are translucent and slightly browned. Reduce the heat to medium-low and stir in the mushrooms, eggplant, garlic, and water. Cover and cook 10 minutes or until the eggplant is softened.

Stir in the olives, rosemary, and chopped roasted red peppers. Cook, uncovered, for 5 minutes. Remove from the heat.

The sauce can be served warm or cold, as a stand-alone dip or as a sauce for anything from beef to noodles to pizza. It makes a great sandwich spread/vegetarian paté if you run it through a food processor. The sauce can be refrigerated for up to 5 days or frozen for up to 3 months.

Yield: 3 cups (675 g)

■ CUMIN-SCENTED GUACAMOLE

Nut-Free, Dairy-Free, Soy-Free, Egg-Free, Vegetarian, 20 minutes or less

It's the classic cilantro question: Should you include the stems, or should you just use the leaves? I say it's situation-dependent. If your bunch of cilantro is very fresh and the stems are thin, use them. If your cilantro has been sitting around a while and the stems are thick and woody-feeling, I say pluck the leaves free and discard the stems. But it's up to you.

Recipe Note
....

➤ If you love the flavor of cumin, go ahead and add 1 full teaspoon to your gua- camole. If you're not a cumin lover, scale it back to ¼ tea- spoon or omit it altogether.

2 ripe avocados, pitted and peeled
2 large tomatoes, chopped
4 green onions, green part only, minced
1 clove garlic, minced

Handful of cilantro, chopped
Juice of half a lemon or lime
½ teaspoon cumin (See Recipe Note)
Pinch of sea salt

Place the avocado in a bowl and use a fork to smash it into a smooth paste. Stir in the remaining ingredients, then taste to see if you'd like to add more lemon or lime juice or a little more salt. Serve with veggies or tortilla chips or use instead of mayo on sandwiches and burgers.

To store the guacamole in the fridge, smooth the top with the back of a spoon and lightly press a piece of plastic wrap onto the top so that no air is touching the guacamole. Stored this way, guacamole will last for up to 4 days in the fridge. If any surface browning does occur, scrape it off with the edge of a spoon or knife before enjoying the guacamole.

Yield: about 2 cups (450 g)

■ SWEET MANGO-PINEAPPLE SALSA

Nut-Free, Dairy-Free, Soy-Free, Egg-Free, Vegetarian, 20 minutes or less

This salsa works well with everything from seafood and fish to chicken and veggies! Try using it in place of marinara to give a Mexican flair to a dish that you'd normally serve in an Italian spirit, or simply serve the salsa with corn chips.

2 green onions, green part only, minced
2 champagne mangoes or 1 standard mango, peeled, pitted, and chopped

1 cup chopped fresh pineapple
1 clove garlic, minced
1 tablespoon (15 ml) fresh lime juice
Handful of fresh cilantro, chopped

Place all the ingredients in a nonreactive bowl (glass works best) and stir gently to combine. The salsa can be refrigerated for up to 4 days.

Yield: about 2 cups (454 g)

◀ NUT & SEED BALLS

Dairy-Free, Soy-Free, Egg-Free, Vegetarian, 20 minutes or less

Not only are these quick-and-easy snacks great for—well, snacking—but they're also instant salad toppers. Just crumble them onto some mixed greens and toss with extra-virgin olive oil and a splash of vinegar. You'll have a nut-tossed, raisin-scented, seed-bejeweled, coconut-crowned salad to enjoy in less than a minute!

½ cup (73 g) roasted sunflower or pumpkin seeds
¼ cup (35 g) raisins or chopped dates
½ cup (130 g) almond or peanut butter, chilled

¾ cup (64 g) unsweetened flaked coconut
2 tablespoons (40 g) honey
1 teaspoon cinnamon

Use a coffee/spice grinder to grind the seeds into a coarse flour. Use your hands to mix all the ingredients together in a large mixing bowl. Shape into 1-inch (2.5 cm) balls and store in the refrigerator until they've all been eaten. These nutty treats can be refrigerated for up to 1 week.

Yield: approximately 2 dozen balls

◀ PUMPKIN-MAPLE DIP WITH APPLES & PEARS

Nut-Free (use vanilla), Soy-Free, Egg-Free, Vegetarian, 20 minutes or less

If you want an extra-thick dip, place the yogurt in a colander and suspend within a large mixing bowl. Cover and refrigerate overnight. In the morning, you'll have homemade cream cheese to mix with the pumpkin, maple, and spices.

2 cups (460 g) plain whole-milk Greek yogurt*
1 cup (245 g) canned pumpkin or 1 ½ cups (368 g)
    canned pumpkin if you strain the yogurt overnight
1 teaspoon vanilla or ½ teaspoon hazelnut or
    almond extract

1 teaspoon cinnamon
Maple syrup, to taste
Cut-up pears and apples for dipping
*See Notes on page 41

Stir together all the ingredients except the fruit in a mixing bowl, adding the syrup 1 tablespoon (15 ml) at a time until your dip is sweetened to taste. Add more extract and cinnamon if you'd like. Serve with the apples and pears (or just about any fresh fruit) for dipping. If you're going to be prepping the fruit in advance, swirl the cut apples and pears in a bowl filled with cool water and a squeeze of fresh lemon juice. Leave the fruit submerged until you're ready to arrange it neatly on a serving plate.

Yield: about 3 cups (700 g)

■ MULTISEED MULTIGRAIN CRACKERS

Nut-Free, Dairy-Free, Soy-Free, Egg-Free, Vegetarian

For the topping seeds, use sesame, poppy, flax, and/or caraway. For the flours, opt for cornmeal that does not say "degerminated"—degerminated cornmeal has had the germ removed, and the germ is the most nutritious part of the cornmeal! As for the bean flour, either fava bean or chickpea flour works, although fava bean flour has a smoother, more mild flavor.

For the topping:
¼ cup (36 g) assorted seeds
1 teaspoon coarse sea salt
1 tablespoon (3 g) dried herbs, such as basil,
   rosemary, thyme, sage, or dill
Freshly ground pepper

For the cracker dough:
¼ cup (32 g) plantain flour or corn
   flour* (not cornstarch)
¼ cup (42 g) whole cornmeal*
½ cup (80 g) brown rice flour
½ cup (70 g) fava bean flour or
   chickpea flour
1 teaspoon sea salt
1 tablespoon (15 ml) extra-virgin
   olive oil
½ cup (120 ml) water, or more as needed
See Notes on page 41

Preheat the oven to 450°F (230°C, or gas mark 8)—crackers are a fast and hot oven job! Cover a baking sheet with parchment paper.

To make the topping: Combine the ingredients in a small bowl and set aside.

To make the dough: Whisk the flours and sea salt together in a large bowl. Add the oil and water and stir until you have a firm dough that isn't too wet but also isn't crumbly: You should be able to easily shape the dough into balls. If the dough is too crumbly, trickle in more water to reach the right consistency, adding 1 tablespoon (15 ml) at a time.

Divide the dough into 4 small balls and work with one at a time. Place a ball on the parchment-covered sheet and pat down to flatten. Sprinkle the dough with the topping. Use a rolling pin to roll out the dough directly onto the parchment, adding more seeds if the dough starts sticking to the rolling pin. Gently flip the dough and repeat the procedure on the other side. When the disk is flattened to a rectangle that's about ¼ inch (6 mm) thick (it'll take up about one-quarter of the baking sheet), slide the disk into one corner of the sheet and repeat the process with the other 3 balls of dough. Press the quarters loosely together before baking.

Bake the crackers for 7 to 10 minutes. When the edges start to brown and the cracker is turning golden, remove from the oven and let cool on a wire rack. As soon as the crackers are cool enough to touch, break them up into smaller crackers with your hands.

Yield: 1 15 ¼ x 10 ¼- inch (40 x 25 cm) cracker

■ BUTTERY CHEDDAR-SAGE CRACKERS

Soy-Free, Egg-Free, Vegetarian

Parchment paper, how many ways do gluten-free bakers love thee? You make everything possible: crackers that we can lift and break apart without a second thought, muffins that come free of their cups with nary a crumb wasted, cookies that slide free from their baking sheets and into our cookie jars. With you, parchment paper, we need not fear The Sundering of Our Baked Goods. You are as indispensible as eggs and mixing bowls.

1 cup (116 g) gluten-free oat flour
½ cup (80 g) millet or brown rice flour
½ cup plus 2 tablespoons (100 g) almond flour
1 teaspoon baking powder*
1 tablespoon (2 g) ground dried sage

¾ teaspoon sea salt
2 cups (240 g) finely shredded Cheddar cheese*
4 tablespoons (55 g) salted butter*
¼ cup (60 ml) water
See Notes on page 41

Preheat the oven to 350°F (180°C, or gas mark 4) and cover a baking sheet with parchment paper.

Place the flours, baking powder, sage, salt, and Cheddar into a large bowl and whisk until well blended. Cut in the butter with a pastry cutter or 2 knives. Add the water and form into a ball with your hands.

Place a sheet of plastic wrap on top of the dough, then roll it out on the parchment-covered baking sheet. Pull off any ragged edges and re-press them back along the edges to form as neat a rectangle as possible.

Press the edge of a clean ruler into the dough to score it into 2-inch (5 cm) squares, first scoring horizontal lines and then scoring the vertical ones. Bake the crackers for 15 minutes, or until the edges are golden brown.

Let the crackers cool before using the edge of a stiff spatula to gently press down on the score lines to break/cut the baked dough into square crackers. Store completely cooled crackers in an airtight tin for up to 4 days.

Yield: approximately 2 dozen crackers

HOMEMADE SODAS

Nut-Free, Dairy-Free, Soy-Free, Egg-Free, Vegetarian, 20 minutes or less

We all know that sugary soda is a bad idea . . . but many of us crave fizzy refreshment. Time to make our own sodas!

■ ORANGE-VANILLA

2 to 4 tablespoons (28 to 60 ml) fresh orange juice

8 ounces (235 ml) plain sparkling water
Drizzle of vanilla extract

Gently stir the freshly squeezed orange juice into a glass of sparkling water. Add the vanilla (a little goes a long way!) and stir.

Yield: 1 serving

■ CRANBERRY-LIME

2 tablespoons (28 ml) unsweetened cranberry juice
Juice of ¼ lime
1 tablespoon (28 ml) maple syrup or 2 teaspoons (13 g) honey, or sweetened to taste

8 ounces (235 ml) plain sparkling water

Combine the cranberry juice, lime juice, and maple syrup in a glass, stirring briskly. If you use honey, you'll have to stir a little longer—it doesn't dissolve as readily as maple syrup does. Either option works, although the maple syrup will lend the drink a decidedly maple flavor, whereas the honey provides more of a general sweetness. Add the sparkling water and stir gently to combine.

Yield: 1 serving

HOT CHOCOLATES: TRADITIONAL, CINNAMON-ALMOND & GINGERED TROPICAL

Prefab hot chocolate is more about artificial flavors and fillers than chocolate. The solution? Make your own hot chocolate using unsweetened cocoa powder and maple syrup. You can customize your warm chocolate treat to your heart's content by experimenting with various extracts and different types of milk.

◼ TRADITIONAL

Nut-Free, Soy-Free, Egg-Free, Vegetarian, 20 minutes or less

2 tablespoons (10 g) unsweetened cocoa powder*
1 tablespoon (15 ml) maple syrup or brown rice syrup
Boiling water

2 to 4 tablespoons (28 to 60 ml) whole milk*
½ teaspoon vanilla extract
See Notes on page 41

Place the cocoa and maple syrup in a mug. Fill halfway with boiling water and stir until smooth. Top off with the milk and stir in the vanilla.

Yield: 1 serving

◼ CINNAMON-ALMOND

Soy-Free, Egg-Free, Vegetarian, 20 minutes or less

2 tablespoons (10 g) unsweetened cocoa powder*
1 tablespoon (15 ml) maple syrup or brown rice syrup
½ teaspoon cinnamon
Boiling water

2 to 4 tablespoons (28 to 60 ml) whole milk*
¼ teaspoon almond extract
See Notes on page 41

Place the cocoa, maple syrup, and cinnamon in a mug. Fill halfway with boiling water and stir until smooth. Top off with the milk and stir in the almond extract.

Yield: 1 serving

◼ GINGERED TROPICAL

Dairy-Free, Soy-Free, Egg-Free, Vegetarian, 20 minutes or less

2 tablespoons (10 g) unsweetened cocoa powder*
1 tablespoon (15 ml) palm sugar or brown rice syrup
½ teaspoon ground ginger

Boiling water
2 tablespoons to ¼ cup (28 to 60 ml) coconut milk
½ teaspoon vanilla extract
See Notes on page 41

Place the cocoa, palm sugar, and ginger in a mug. Fill halfway with boiling water and stir until smooth. Top off with the coconut milk and stir in vanilla.

Yield: 1 serving

Chapter 11 | Cakes, Cookies & Other Sweet Endings: Baking Gluten-Free and Whole-Grain!

While having dessert for dinner isn't a great idea, making your desserts healthier by using whole-grain flours and natural sweeteners is a fantastic idea! The treats you'll find in this chapter feature a wide variety of unrefined ingredients to satisfy your sweet tooth, whether you're in the mood for ice cream or brownies or something more exotic. Dessert tastes even better when you can feel good about eating it!

■ YOU-WON'T-BELIEVE-IT'S-WHOLE-GRAIN CINNAMON & MAPLE CHOCOLATE CUPCAKES

Soy-Free, Vegetarian

These dark chocolate cupcakes are for die-hard chocolate lovers. If you'd prefer sweeter 'cakes, use ¾ cup (175 ml) of maple syrup rather than ½ cup (120 ml). And for a soft texture, use freshly ground almond flour—it's fluffier and moister than preground almond flour.

For the cupcakes:
1 ¼ cups (112 g) almond flour (See Recipe Note)
¼ cup (30 g) raw buckwheat or teff flour
½ cup (40 g) unsweetened cocoa powder*
½ teaspoon baking powder*
¼ teaspoon baking soda
1 ½ teaspoons cinnamon
½ cup (120 ml) maple syrup
4 tablespoons (55 g) butter, melted*

2 eggs*
¾ cup (175 ml) whole milk*
1 teaspoon vanilla extract

For the frosting:
1 ½ cups (360 g) mascarpone cheese*
¼ cup (60 ml) maple syrup, or more to taste
½ teaspoon vanilla extract
See Notes on page 41

Preheat the oven to 375ºF (190ºC, or gas mark 5) and line a muffin tin with 12 parchment paper muffin cups. Set aside.

To make the cupcakes: In a large bowl, whisk together the flours, cocoa, baking powder, baking soda, and cinnamon. In a smaller bowl, whisk together the remaining ingredients. Stir the wet ingredients into the dry ingredients until well blended. Fill each muffin cup about three-quarters full. Bake for 25 minutes, or until a toothpick inserted into the center of the center-most cupcake comes out clean and warm.

To make the frosting: Stir together the mascarpone cheese, maple syrup, and vanilla in a small bowl. Taste it to see whether you'd like it to be a little sweeter. If so, add another 1 tablespoon (15 ml) of maple syrup. Frost each completely cooled cupcake with a spoonful of the frosting, gently swirling the frosting across the top of the cupcake with the back of the spoon. Sprinkle with just a dash of cinnamon if you'd like—it makes a gorgeous contrast against the light-colored frosting. Frosted cupcakes can be refrigerated for up to 5 days.

Yield: 12 cupcakes

> **Recipe Note**
> ....
> ➤ To make almond flour, run sliced almonds through a coffee/spice grinder for about 10 seconds.

■ PEACH-SWIRLED CHEESECAKE

Soy-Free, Vegetarian

Peach and apricot jam work equally well in this cheesecake. Whichever you choose, look for a naturally sweetened, no-sugar-added jam. Use ½ cup (160 g) jam for a more savory cheesecake or up to 1 cup (320 g) jam for a sweeter, more fruity cake.

For the crust:
1 cup (90 g) almond flour, plus more for dusting
½ cup (60 g) raw buckwheat flour or brown rice flour
¼ cup (29 g) oat flour (See Recipe Note)
1 teaspoon cinnamon
½ cup (112 g) butter*

For the filling:
3 eggs*
3 cups (690 g) homemade cream cheese* (see sidebar)
¼ cup (40 g) powdered sucanat (See Recipe Note)
2 teaspoons (10 ml) vanilla extract
½ to 1 cup (160 to 320 g) naturally sweetened peach or apricot jam, plus more for topping
See Notes on page 41

Preheat the oven to 400°F (200°C, or gas mark 6).

To make the crust: Briefly blend the flours and cinnamon in a food processor. Add the butter in chunks and blend again. The butter will begin to form crumbs with the flour, and then it'll suddenly wham itself into a ball. Stop!

Pat the dough into the bottom of a 9- or 10-inch (23 or 25 cm) springform pan, dusting your hands with almond flour if the dough sticks. Bake for 20 minutes. Remove to a wire rack and let cool slightly. Reduce the oven temperature to 375°F (190°C, or gas mark 5).

To make the filling: Place the eggs, cream cheese, sucanat, and vanilla in a large bowl. Whisk vigorously to blend well. Add the jam and whisk just a few times—you want some streaks. Pour into the springform pan.

Bake for 30 minutes. Reduce the heat to 325°F (170°C, or gas mark 3) and bake an additional 30 minutes. The cake will be jiggly in the center, brown around the edges, and there will be a few bubbles on the surface.

Let the cake cool completely. Unsnap the springform pan and serve slices topped with a dollop of jam. Leftover cake can be refrigerated for up to 5 days.

Yield: one 9- or 10-inch (23 or 25 cm) cheesecake

Recipe Notes
....

➤ Make powdered sucanat by running sucanat through a coffee/spice grinder until powdery.

➤ Use a coffee/spice grinder to grind gluten-free rolled oats into flour.

EASY CREAM CHEESE
....

2 cups (460 g) plain whole-milk Greek yogurt*
See Notes on page 41

The night before, scoop yogurt into a colander suspended over a large mixing bowl. Cover with plastic wrap and refrigerate overnight. In the morning, you'll have cream cheese!

Yield: 1 ¼ cups (290 g)

■ ALMOND SPONGE CAKE WITH CHOCOLATE GANACHE FROSTING

Soy-Free, Vegetarian

While making this cake—or any cake with whipped egg whites—do not clonk things on the counter or against the mixing bowl! Clonking will deflate your whipped eggs and lessen your lift, resulting in a flatter cake. I put a towel on the counter so that I can set things down softly.

For the cake:
2 egg yolks*
5 whole eggs*
½ cup (80 g) powdered sucanat (See Recipe Note)
1 teaspoon vanilla extract
1 cup (90 g) almond flour
⅓ cup (48 g) sorghum flour
2 teaspoons (9 g) baking powder*

6 tablespoons (85 g) butter, melted and cooled*

For the frosting:
3 ½ ounces (100 g) 75% to 85% dark chocolate
½ cup (120 ml) heavy cream, chilled*
See Notes on page 41

Recipe Notes
....

➤ Make powdered sucanat by running sucanat through a coffee/spice grinder until powdery.

➤ When you refrigerate the cake for more than a few hours, the ganache frosting will harden, so it's best to let any leftover slices sit out at room temperature for an hour to soften before serving.

Preheat the oven to 325°F (170°C, or gas mark 3) and thoroughly grease an 8 x 8-inch (20 x 20 cm) glass pan.

To make the cake: Place the egg yolks, eggs, sucanat, and vanilla in a large mixing bowl. Whip on high for 4 full minutes with a hand mixer or a standing mixer. Quickly whip in the flours, baking powder, and melted butter. Pour the batter into the pan and bake for 30 minutes, or until a toothpick inserted into the center of the cake comes out clean and warm. Let the cake cool before frosting.

To make the frosting: Place a large mixing bowl and the beaters in the freezer. Break up the chocolate and place in a small saucepan over the lowest heat setting. Melt slowly, stirring often. Remove from the heat when the chocolate still has a few lumps and continue stirring to finish melting the chocolate. Set aside.

Pour the cream into the chilled bowl and whip with the chilled beaters until you have fluffy but still smooth cream. Whip in the melted chocolate.

Frost the cooled cake and refrigerate for at least 30 minutes to set the frosting. Leftover cake can be refrigerated for up to 4 days.

Yield: one 8 x 8-inch (20 x 20 cm) cake

■ VANILLA CHIFFON CAKE WITH FRESH STRAWBERRIES & WHIPPED CREAM

Nut-Free, Soy-Free, Vegetarian

Chiffon cakes are all about eggs. Eggs from free-range hens are stronger than conventional eggs, which means they provide a stronger structure. Stronger structure = taller, lighter cakes. Free-range eggs are worth seeking out!

1 cup (120 g) raw buckwheat or
   sorghum flour
½ cup (80 g) millet flour
½ cup (80 g) brown rice flour
¾ cup plus 2 tablespoons (123 g)
   powdered sucanat (See Recipe
   Note)
1 tablespoon (14 g) baking powder*
¼ teaspoon sea salt
6 egg yolks, at room temperature*

1 cup (235 ml) whole milk*
¼ cup (60 ml) extra-virgin olive oil
2 teaspoons (10 ml) vanilla extract
8 egg whites, at room temperature*
½ teaspoon cream of tartar
Sliced fresh strawberries*
Freshly whipped cream*
   (see page 163)
See Notes on page 41

Recipe Note

➤ Make powdered sucanat by running sucanat through a coffee/spice grinder until powdery.

Preheat the oven to 325°F (170°C, or gas mark 3). Set aside an ungreased 10-inch (25 cm) tube pan.

In a medium bowl, whisk together flours, ¾ cup (105 g) of the powdered sucanat, the baking powder, and the salt. In another medium bowl, briefly beat the egg yolks, milk, oil, and vanilla. Add the flour mixture and beat for at least 2 minutes.

Place the egg whites in a large bowl. Sprinkle with the cream of tartar and whip the egg whites until they're fluffy and form smooth peaks. Sprinkle on the remaining 2 tablespoons (18 g) powdered sucanat and continue to whip until the whites are glossy and firm peaks form.

With a spatula, gently fold half of the cake mixture into the whites. After about 10 folding strokes, fold in the remaining batter. (To fold, scoop the spatula along the bottom of the bowl and lift the spatula toward you, then back down in a circular motion while rotating the bowl with your other hand.) Pour into the tube pan and bake for 1 hour, or until the top is golden brown and a toothpick inserted near the center comes out clean and warm.

Let the cake cool upside down. When the cake is completely cool, run a thin spatula along the outer and inner ring of the tube pan, then wriggle the spatula underneath the cake to help pull it free. Or cut the cake in half with a very sharp knife and lift it out in 2 pieces.

Serve slices of cake with the strawberries and whipped cream, topping each slice as you serve it. Leftover cake can be refrigerated for up to 5 days.

Yield: one 10-inch (25 cm) tube cake

■ CHOCOLATE ANGEL FOOD CAKE WITH SMASHED RASPBERRY GLAZE

Nut-Free, Dairy-Free, Soy-Free, Vegetarian

This raspberry glaze is delicious on everything from cakes to ice cream to pancakes. Try swapping out the raspberries for frozen blueberries or strawberries, or make a mixed-berry glaze.

Recipe Note

➤ As it cooks down, the glaze has a tendency to bubble up and splatter out of the pot. Do not reach over the pot at any time.

For the cake:
½ cup (40 g) unsweetened cocoa
  powder*
½ cup (80 g) brown rice flour
½ cup (70 g) powdered sucanat
  (see Recipe Note on page 141)
10 egg whites, at room temperature*
1 teaspoon lemon juice
2 tablespoons (28 ml) water
2 teaspoons (10 ml) vanilla extract
1 teaspoon cream of tartar

For the glaze:
12 ounces (340 g) frozen raspberries
½ cup (120 ml) water
2 tablespoons (28 ml) maple syrup
See Notes on page 41

Preheat the oven to 350°F (180°C, or gas mark 4). Set out an ungreased 10-inch (25 cm) tube pan.

To make the cake: In a medium bowl, whisk together the cocoa powder, flour, and ¼ cup (35 g) of the sucanat. Set aside.

In a large mixing bowl, whip the egg whites, lemon juice, water, vanilla, and cream of tartar until they're fluffy and forming smooth peaks. Sprinkle half of the cocoa-and-flour mixture on top of the whipped eggs and gently fold in the mixture with a spatula. After about 10 folding strokes, fold in the remaining cocoa mixture. (To fold, scoop the spatula along the bottom of the bowl and lift the spatula toward you, then back down in a circular motion while rotating the bowl with your other hand.) Pour into the pan and bake for 40 minutes, or until a toothpick inserted near the center comes out clean and warm.

Let the cake cool upside down. When the cake is completely cool, run a thin spatula along the outer and inner ring of the tube pan, then wriggle the spatula underneath the cake to pull it free. Or cut the cake in half with a very sharp knife and lift it out in 2 pieces.

To make the glaze: Place all the ingredients in a small pot over medium-low heat. Simmer for 10 minutes, then smash the raspberries with a potato masher. Reduce the heat to low and simmer for 30 minutes, or until the glaze is reduced by half. Remove from the heat and let cool.

When serving, top each slice with a spoonful of glaze. The leftover cake and glaze can be refrigerated separately for up to 5 days.

Yield: one 10-inch (25 cm) tube cake

■ FIVE-MINUTE CHESTNUT FUDGE CAKE

Soy-Free, Dairy-Free (use coconut milk), Vegetarian

Look for roasted and peeled chestnuts in the baking section or near the canned fruit—round, whole chestnuts are sold vacuum-sealed and boxed or in jars. Be sure to buy whole unsweetened chestnuts.

2 ounces (55 g) 75% to 85% dark chocolate, broken
   into chunks
8 ounces (225 g) steamed unsweetened chestnuts
1 egg*
¼ cup (60 ml) maple syrup
¼ cup (60 ml) buttermilk, whole milk, or coconut milk

1 teaspoon vanilla extract
Pinch of sea salt
1 tablespoon (14 g) baking powder*
No-sugar-added raspberry jam, for topping
Whipped cream, for topping* (see page 163)
See Notes on page 41

Preheat the oven to 350°F (180°C, or gas mark 4). Grease a 9-inch (23 cm) glass pie pan and set aside.

In a small pot, melt the chocolate over the lowest heat setting, whisking often to help the chocolate melt. Remove from the heat and whisk away the last lumps.

Pour the melted chocolate into a food processor. Add the remaining ingredients except for the jam and cream and process until smooth. Pour the batter into the prepared pan and bake for 28 to 30 minutes, or until the center is firm and set. Serve with the jam and a dollop of whipped cream. The cake can be refrigerated for up to 5 days, although it's best when served warm.

Yield: one 9-inch (23 cm) cake

■ ORANGE-COCONUT CAKE

Soy-Free, Vegetarian

Look for coconut nectar in health-food stores. Not only does it have a pleasantly caramel-like flavor, but it also tastes sweeter than brown rice syrup, so you don't need as much to achieve the same level of sweetness. Plus, using coconut nectar for this cake means you're using coconut in every possible way: flaked coconut, coconut milk, coconut oil, coconut flour, and coconut nectar!

For the cake:
1 cup (85 g) unsweetened coconut flakes
½ cup (70 g) coconut flour
½ cup (80 g) brown rice flour
1 cup (90 g) almond flour
1 teaspoon baking powder*
Pinch of sea salt
½ cup (80 g) sucanat
½ cup (112 g) butter, melted*
2 eggs*
½ cup (120 ml) whole coconut milk
1 teaspoon vanilla extract
Juice and zest of 1 large orange*
   (about ⅓ cup [80 ml] juice)

For the icing:
1 cup (235 ml) coconut milk
½ cup (120 ml) melted coconut oil
2 teaspoons (10 ml) vanilla extract
2 tablespoons (28 ml) coconut nectar or ¼ cup
   (60 ml) brown rice syrup
See Notes on page 41

Preheat the oven to 350°F (180°C, or gas mark 4) and thoroughly grease an 8 x 8-inch (20 x 20 cm) pan.

To make the cake: Heat the coconut flakes in a large skillet over medium heat. Toast for about 5 minutes, stirring occasionally, or until the coconut is fragrant and turning light brown. Immediately remove from the heat and transfer to a cool plate.

In a large bowl, whisk together the flours, baking powder, salt, and sucanat. Add ½ cup (43 g) of the toasted coconut. In another bowl, whisk together the butter, eggs, coconut milk, vanilla, and orange juice and zest. Stir the wet ingredients into the dry ingredients, stirring until well blended. Pour into the greased pan and bake for 30 minutes, or until a toothpick inserted into the center comes out clean.

To make the icing: Whisk together all the ingredients and refrigerate for 1 hour before spooning the frosting onto the cake. Sprinkle with the remaining ½ cup (43 g) toasted coconut flakes. Leftover cake can be refrigerated for up to 4 days.

Yield: one 8 x 8-inch (20 x 20 cm) cake

■ SPICED MESQUITE & SORGHUM COFFEE CAKE

Soy-Free, Vegetarian

Ever grilled with mesquite chips? The same tree bears edible pods that can be dried and then ground into flour. Like the wood, the pods have a pronounced caramel/molasses flavor that pairs beautifully with spices such as cinnamon and cardamom.

For the streusel:
¼ cup (30 g) mesquite flour
¼ cup (40 g) sucanat
1 teaspoon cinnamon
½ teaspoon cardamom
½ teaspoon allspice
Generous 1 cup (120 g) chopped walnuts or pecans
6 tablespoons (85 g) butter, chilled*

For the cake:
¾ cup (120 g) millet flour
¾ cup (150 g) teff or brown rice flour
½ cup (70 g) sorghum flour
½ teaspoon cardamom
1 teaspoon ginger
1 teaspoon baking soda
1 teaspoon baking powder*
½ cup (112 g) butter, softened*
1 teaspoon vanilla or lemon extract
4 eggs*
½ cup (170 g) honey
1 cup (230) plain whole-milk plain Greek yogurt*
*See Notes on page 41

Preheat the oven to 350°F (180°C, or gas mark 4). Grease a 10-inch (25 cm) tube pan with butter and then dust it with millet or brown rice flour: Sprinkle on some flour and then turn the pan sideways, tapping and turning it to dust the sides as well as the bottom. Set aside.

To make the streusel: Whisk together all of the ingredients except the butter. Use a pastry cutter (or 2 knives in a crisscross motion) to cut the butter into the flour mixture to create small crumbs. Refrigerate the streusel while you make the cake.

To make the cake: In a medium bowl, whisk together the flours, spices, baking soda, and baking powder. In a large bowl, cream the butter with the vanilla for at least 2 minutes, or until the butter has become pale and fluffy. Beat in the eggs one at a time. Beat in the honey and yogurt, and then beat in the flour mixture.

Pour half of the batter into the prepared pan. Sprinkle on half of the streusel. Finish pouring in the batter and top the cake with the remaining streusel. Bake for 50 to 60 minutes, or until a toothpick inserted near the center comes out clean and warm.

Let the cake cool completely on a wire rack before running a spatula around the edges to loosen the cake from the pan. Leftover cake can be refrigerated for up to 5 days. If you like, serve the cake with a dollop of yogurt and a drizzle of honey, or drizzle with unrefined walnut or pecan oil.

Yield: one-10 inch (25 cm) tube cake

■ ULTRA-DARK OAT & DATE BROWNIES

Soy-Free, Vegetarian

Don't throw away your butter wrappers! Whenever you use a stick of butter and you're left with just the wrapper, fold it in half to protect the butter still clinging to it, then stash it in your fridge with any remaining sticks. The next time you need to grease a pan, use one of your buttery wrappers. Waste not, want not!

½ cup (112 g) butter*
¾ cup (175 ml) unrefined hazelnut oil or extra-virgin olive oil
¾ cup (120 g) sucanat
6 dates, pitted, at room temperature
¾ cup (48 g) cocoa powder*
½ cup (100 g) teff flour
½ cup (70 g) coconut flour

½ cup (70 g) sorghum flour
1 teaspoon baking powder*
Pinch of sea salt
½ cup (40 g) gluten-free rolled oats
6 eggs*
1 teaspoon vanilla extract
See Notes on page 41

Preheat the oven to 350°F (180°C, or gas mark 4) and grease an 8 x 8-inch (20 x 20 cm) glass baking pan with butter.

Place the butter in a medium pot over low heat and melt. Stir in the oil, sucanat, and dates. Mash with a potato masher until the dates are mostly smooth. Stir in the cocoa powder and transfer to a large mixing bowl. Let cool while you whisk together the flours, baking powder, salt, and oats in another bowl.

Whisk the eggs and vanilla into the cocoa mixture. With a large mixing spoon, mix the flours into the cocoa mixture. Pour the batter into the prepared pan and bake for 40 minutes, or until a toothpick inserted into the center comes out clean and warm. The brownies can be refrigerated for up to 1 week.

Yield: one 8 x 8-inch (20 x 20 cm) pan

■ DOUBLE CHOCOLATE CRUNCH COOKIES

Soy-Free, Vegetarian

Yes, here's another recipe for all the dark chocolate lovers. This time, we've got cocoa powder and nibs! If you're a dark chocolate fan, use ¾ cup (120 g) sucanat to allow the cocoa flavor to shine through in these cookies; if you would like your cookies to be sweeter, use 1 cup (160 g) sucanat.

1 cup (120 g) pecan or walnut halves
½ cup (70 g) sorghum flour
½ cup (80 g) brown rice flour
½ cup (80 g) millet or amaranth flour
½ cup (40 g) cocoa powder*
2 teaspoons (9 g) baking powder*

1 cup (225 g) butter*
¾ to 1 cup (120 to 160 g) sucanat
2 teaspoons (10 ml) vanilla extract
2 eggs*
½ cup (72 g) raw or toasted cocoa nibs
See Notes on page 41

Position 2 oven racks in the upper and lower thirds of the oven. Preheat oven to 325°F (170°C, or gas mark 3). Cover 2 baking sheets with parchment paper.

Coarsely chop the pecans and place them in a large skillet. Toast them over medium-low heat, stirring occasionally, for 4 to 5 minutes, or until they're fragrant and turning brown. (All of a sudden, the air will smell like pecans. A lot like pecans.) Slide the pecans onto a plate and set aside.

Whisk the flours, cocoa powder, and baking powder together in a medium bowl and set aside. In a large mixing bowl, cream the butter for 2 minutes, or until it's light and fluffy. Gradually beat in the sucanat. Add the vanilla and 1 of the eggs and beat again. Beat in the remaining egg.

Use a wooden spoon to stir in the flour mixture, then the nibs and the toasted nuts. Use a spoon to drop 1-inch (2.5 cm) rounds of batter onto the baking sheets, putting about 20 cookies on one sheet. Leave a bit of space between the cookies to allow them to spread as they bake.

Bake for 10 to 12 minutes, switching racks halfway through, or until the cookies are fragrant and starting to crack slightly. Let the sheets cool on wire racks before baking the second round of cookies. (You can reuse the parchment paper.) Completely cooled cookies can be stored in an airtight container at room temperature for about 1 week.

Yield: about 6 dozen cookies

■ PEANUT BUTTER CINNAMON COOKIES

Soy-Free, Vegetarian

When it comes to peanut butter, be sure to choose one that's just peanuts (or peanuts and salt). For this recipe, I prefer to use creamy salted organic peanut butter made of Valencia peanuts, but you could just as easily opt for crunchy unsalted peanut butter. If your peanut butter is already salted, omit the 1/2 teaspoon sea salt.

1/4 cup (55 g) butter, melted*
1/4 cup (60 ml) unrefined peanut oil
1/2 cup (125 g) unsweetened applesauce*
1 cup (260 g) natural peanut butter
1/4 cup (40 g) sucanat
2 eggs*
1/4 cup (85 g) honey
1/2 teaspoon sea salt if using unsalted peanut butter

2 teaspoons (5 g) cinnamon, plus extra for
  sprinkling if desired
1 tablespoon (14 g) baking powder*
1/2 cup (80 g) brown rice flour
3/4 cup (120 g) amaranth flour
1/2 cup (100 g) teff flour
1/2 cup (70 g) sorghum flour
See Notes on page 41

Position 2 oven racks in the upper and lower thirds of the oven. Preheat the oven to 350°F (180°C, or gas mark 4) and line 2 baking sheets with parchment paper.

In a large bowl, whisk together the butter, peanut oil, applesauce, and peanut butter. Add the sucanat, eggs, and honey. Whisk again to thoroughly combine.

In a medium bowl, whisk together the sea salt, cinnamon, baking powder, and flours. Stir the wet ingredients into the dry ingredients until well blended.

Use a spoon to drop 1-inch (2.5 cm) rounds of batter onto the baking sheets. If you want them round and poufy, leave them as they are; if you want your cookies to be a bit flatter, press them down lightly with your fingers or a fork (for the classic ridged pattern). Leave a bit of space between the cookies to allow them to spread as they bake.

Bake the cookies for about 10 minutes, switching the racks halfway through, or until the bottoms of the cookies are lightly browned. Let the baking sheets cool slightly on wire racks before baking another round of cookies. (You can reuse the parchment paper.)

Sprinkle additional cinnamon over the cookies just before serving if desired. Completely cooled cookies can be stored in an airtight container at room temperature for about 1 week.

Yield: about 9 dozen cookies

CHESTNUT SNICKERDOODLES WITH PINE NUTS

Soy-Free, Vegetarian

When you switch from conventional butter to butter from grass-fed cows, you notice two things: the grass-fed butter is more yellow, and it's much, much softer. It's so soft, in fact, that you can cream it after you let it stand at room temperature for 10 minutes. If you leave grass-fed butter out for longer than 30 minutes, it gets so soft that when you go to cream it, it'll feel more like it's melting. That's because the cream from grass-fed cows contains much less saturated fat than does the cream from conventional cows, which makes it less stiff. On the flip side, if you need your butter to be well chilled for making a piecrust, leave your grass-fed butter in the refrigerator until the last possible second so that it's as firm as possible.

2 cups (200 g) chestnut flour, or 1 cup (100 g) chestnut
    and 1 cup (100 g) brown rice flour
2 teaspoons (9 g) cream of tartar
1 teaspoon baking soda
2 teaspoons (5 g) cinnamon

1 cup (225 g) butter, softened*
¾ cup (120 g) sucanat
2 eggs*
½ cup (68 g) pine nuts
*See Notes on page 41

Position 2 oven racks in the upper and lower thirds of the oven. Preheat the oven to 350°F (180°C, or gas mark 4) and line 2 baking sheets with parchment paper.

In a medium bowl, whisk together the flour, cream of tartar, baking soda, and cinnamon. In a large bowl, cream the butter with the sucanat for 2 full minutes, or until the butter is very soft and creamy. Beat in the eggs one at a time, then stir in the flour mixture. Stir in the pine nuts.

Use a spoon to drop 1-inch (2.5 cm) rounds of batter onto the baking sheets, using an ordinary teaspoon to ensure uniformly sized cookies. Leave a bit of space between the cookies to allow them to spread as they bake.

Bake for about 12 minutes, switching the racks halfway through, or until the edges are turning golden brown. Let the baking sheets cool on wire racks. Completely cooled cookies can be stored in an airtight container at room temperature for about 1 week.

Yield: about 5 dozen cookies

GINGERSNAPS WITH TEFF & ALMOND

Soy-Free, Vegetarian

These cookies make great miniature ice cream sandwiches—they're equally delicious with the Pumpkin Spice Ice Cream (page 164) or the Blueberry Buttermilk Ice Cream (page 165). Or you can grind the 'snaps into crumbs in a food processor and then use them the same way you'd use graham cracker crumbs, from topping parfaits to making piecrusts.

½ cup (100 g) teff flour
½ cup (45 g) almond flour
¾ cup (120 g) brown rice flour
¾ teaspoon baking powder*
¼ teaspoon baking soda
1 tablespoon (5.5 g) ground ginger
1 teaspoon ground cinnamon
¼ teaspoon ground cloves

Pinch of sea salt
6 tablespoons (85 g) butter*
¾ cup (120 g) sucanat
1 egg*
¼ cup (85 g) blackstrap molasses
1 teaspoon freshly squeezed lemon juice
See Notes on page 41

Position 2 oven racks in the upper and lower thirds of the oven. Preheat the oven to 350°F (180°C, or gas mark 4). Line 2 baking sheets with parchment paper.

In a medium bowl, whisk together the flours, baking powder, baking soda, spices, and salt. Set aside.

In a large bowl, cream the butter for 2 minutes, or until it has turned pale and creamy. Beat in the sucanat for at least 1 minute, then beat in the egg for another minute. Beat in the molasses and lemon juice until the dough is well blended. Add about half of the flour mixture and beat on medium speed until you have a smooth dough. Repeat with the remaining half of the flour mixture.

Use a spoon to drop 1-inch (2.5 cm) rounds of batter onto the baking sheets. Leave a bit of space between the cookies to allow them to spread as they bake.

Bake the cookies for 12 minutes, switching racks halfway through, or until they're brown around the edges. Remove from the oven and let cool on racks. If any of the cookies have spread into each other, immediately and gently separate them by pressing down on their seams with the edge of a flexible spatula. Allow the cookies to cool completely before removing them from the baking sheets.

Completely cooled cookies can be stored in an airtight container at room temperature for about 1 week.

Yield: about 5 dozen cookies

■ TRAIL MIX COOKIES WITH NIBS

Soy-Free, Vegetarian

Trail mix is one of the easiest and most customizable things to make yourself. All you need to do is combine your favorite nuts (preferably dry-roasted or raw) with your favorite dried fruits (preferably with no sugar added) in any proportion. If you like, you can toss in cocoa nibs, chunks of dark chocolate, flaked raw or toasted coconut, and/or some of your favorite seeds. One of my favorite combos is macadamia nuts with cocoa nibs and raisins. It's the perfect snack to take on a trip . . . or to include in these cookies.

½ cup (80 g) brown rice flour
½ cup (80 g) amaranth or millet
    flour
½ cup (100 g) teff flour
1 teaspoon cinnamon
1 teaspoon baking powder*
Pinch of sea salt
½ cup (112 g) butter, softened*

½ to ¾ cup (80 to 120 g) sucanat,
    plus more for rolling if desired
    (See Recipe Note)
1 egg*
2 teaspoons (10 ml) vanilla extract
1 ½ cups (225 g) trail mix, either
    homemade or store-bought
    (See Recipe Note)
See Notes on page 41

Position 2 oven racks in the upper and lower thirds of the oven. Preheat the oven to 325°F (170°C, or gas mark 3). Line 2 baking sheets with parchment paper.

In a medium bowl, whisk together the flours, cinnamon, baking powder, and salt. In a large mixing bowl, cream the butter for 1 minute, then beat in the sucanat for 1 minute to create a smooth, creamy texture. Beat in the egg and vanilla until well combined. Gradually beat in the flour mixture. Stir in the trail mix by hand.

Use a spoon to drop 1-inch (2.5 cm) rounds of batter onto the baking sheets, leaving space between them. Bake for 15 to 18 minutes, switching racks halfway through, or until golden brown. If you like, you can roll the hot cookies in additional sucanat to give them a sweeter, crunchier exterior. Completely cooled cookies can be stored in an airtight container for up to 5 days.

Yield: about 6 dozen cookies

Recipe Notes

➤ If you'd like your cookies to be more nutty and less sweet, use ½ cup (80 g) sucanat. If you'd like more sweetness than nuttiness, use ¾ cup (120 g) sucanat.

➤ Try to find a trail mix made with unsweetened dried fruit. (Many dried fruits are coated with added sugar.)

Recipe Note

····································

➤ If you don't have 2 cups
(200 g) chestnut flour, substitute 1 cup (100 g) chestnut flour plus 1 cup (140 g)
sorghum flour, or use 2 cups
(280 g) sorghum flour.

■ CHOCOLATE- AND PINE-NUT-STUDDED BISCOTTI

Dairy-Free, Soy-Free, Vegetarian

Pine nuts and dark chocolate are a natural match, albeit one you don't see often. That's a shame, because the soft, creamy flavor of the pine nuts enhances the rich, deep flavor of the dark chocolate. Pine nuts are for more than just pesto!

2 cups (200 g) chestnut flour (See
  Recipe Note)
1 cup (160 g) brown rice flour, plus
  more for dusting
2 ½ teaspoons (11.5 g) baking
  powder*
Pinch of sea salt
4 ounces (115 g) 75% to 85% dark
  chocolate, broken into small pieces

½ cup (68 g) pine nuts, raw or
  toasted
¼ cup (60 ml) extra-virgin olive oil
⅔ cup (110 g) sucanat
3 eggs*
1 teaspoon vanilla extract
See Notes on page 41

Preheat the oven to 375°F (190°C, or gas mark 5). Cover a baking sheet with parchment paper and set aside.

In a large bowl, whisk together the flours, baking powder, salt, chocolate pieces, and pine nuts. In a medium bowl, whisk together the remaining ingredients. Stir the wet ingredients into the dry ones, stirring until well blended.

Flour your hands well with brown rice flour, generously sprinkling more flour onto the dough, and shape the dough into 2 equal logs. Dust your hands with additional flour if the dough insists on sticking to your hands. Each log should stretch across the baking sheet. Bake for 25 minutes.

Let the logs cool on a wire rack for about 5 minutes, then gently slide the baking sheet out from underneath the logs to let the logs sit directly on the wire rack.

In about 10 minutes, the logs should be cool enough to touch comfortably. Cut them into angled slices about ¾ inch (2 cm) thick. Cover 2 baking sheets with parchment paper and arrange the slices on the sheets, spacing them equally apart. Bake for 5 minutes, then pull the sheets out of the oven and carefully flip each slice over. Switch rack positions and bake for another 5 to 8 minutes, or until both sides are golden brown.

Let cool completely before storing the biscotti in an airtight container. The whole point of biscotti is to be bracingly crunchy, and if any moisture forms in the container—which it will if the biscotti are still warm—the crunch will quickly disappear. Keep completely cooled biscotti in an airtight container for up to 1 week.

Yield: about 3 dozen biscotti

■ APPLE PIE WITH NUT & OAT CRUST

Soy-Free, Vegetarian

Making gluten-free crust is easy—the tricky part is rolling it out and laying on the top crust. But as long as you have plenty of plastic wrap on hand, you'll quickly get the hang of it. Serve with shipped cream (page 163).

For the crust:
1 ½ cups (180 g) walnut pieces
1 ¼ cups (138 g) sliced almonds
¾ cup (60 g) gluten-free rolled oats
1 teaspoon cinnamon
½ cup (112 g) butter, well chilled*
1 egg*
1 ¼ cups (150 g) millet or raw buckwheat flour

For the filling:
2 tablespoons (28 g) butter*
5 medium Fuji apples, cored and sliced*
½ teaspoon cinnamon
½ teaspoon nutmeg
½ teaspoon allspice
¼ teaspoon ground cloves
1 teaspoon coriander
2 tablespoons (28 ml) maple syrup, plus more for drizzling if desired
2 teaspoons (10 ml) vanilla extract
¼ cup (29 g) gluten-free oat flour (See Recipe Note)
*See Notes on page 41

Preheat the oven to 375°F (190°C, or gas mark 5). Grease a 10-inch (25 cm) glass pie pan that's 2 inches (5 cm) deep.

To make the crust: Place the nuts, oats, and cinnamon in a food processor and briefly process. Cut the butter into chunks and scatter onto the flour, then briefly process just until crumbs form. Add the egg and process again until the dough balls up against the sides of the processor.

Transfer the dough to a large mixing bowl and knead in the flour. Split the dough into 2 balls. Refrigerate one. Press the other into the bottom and up the sides of the pie pan.

To make the filling: Melt the butter in a large skillet over medium-low heat. Add the apples, spices, and maple syrup. Cover the skillet and cook the apples for 15 minutes, occasionally turning them over. Remove from the heat and stir in the vanilla and oat flour.

Scoop the apples into the bottom crust. Place the refrigerated dough between 2 large sheets of plastic wrap and roll it into a 10-inch (25 cm) circle. Remove the top sheet of plastic wrap. Use the bottom sheet to hold the crust above the pie, then carefully flip the crust onto the apples. Remove the plastic wrap. Pinch the edges together, patching any tears with overhanging pieces of dough. Make 8 slits in the top crust in a sunburst pattern.

Bake the pie for 1 hour, or until the top crust is golden brown and the apples are bubbling. Let cool for at least 15 minutes before cutting into the pie. If desired, drizzle each piece with maple syrup before serving. Leftover pie can be refrigerated for up to 5 days.

Yield: one 10-inch (25 cm) pie

■ PUMPKIN PIE WITH TEFF & PECAN CRUST

Soy-Free, Vegetarian

Fortunately for pecan lovers, pecans are soft enough to easily grind in a food processor. This pie features an ultra-rich spiced pecan crust, ideal for autumn and winter pumpkin pies. If you'd like to make the pie again with a slightly different crust, swap out the pecans for walnut halves. Equally delicious!

For the crust:
1 cup (100 g) pecan halves
⅓ cup (69 g) teff flour
⅓ cup (55 g) brown rice flour
1 teaspoon cinnamon
1 tablespoon (15 ml) maple syrup
4 tablespoons (55 g) butter*

For the filling:
15 ounces (425 g) canned pumpkin
4 eggs*
½ cup (120 ml) maple syrup
¼ cup (60 ml) whole milk*
1 teaspoon cinnamon
½ teaspoon allspice
½ teaspoon ground ginger
¼ teaspoon ground cloves
¼ teaspoon nutmeg
Pinch of sea salt
*See Notes on page 41

Preheat the oven to 400°F (200°C, or gas mark 6) and grease a 10-inch (25 cm) glass pie pan that's 2 inches (5 cm) deep.

To make the crust: Place the pecans, flours, and cinnamon in a food processor and process until you have a fine-crumbed mixture. Add the syrup. Cut the butter into chunks and add the butter. Process again, letting the processor run until the dough comes together into a ball and whumps! against the side of the processor. Stop!

Press the dough into the pan, rolling the dough with the palm of your hand to push the dough up onto the sides. Bake for 10 to 12 minutes, or until the crust is lightly browned. Remove from the oven and decrease the oven temperature to 350°F (180°C, or gas mark 4).

To make the filling: Place all the ingredients into a large mixing bowl and whisk until smooth and well combined.

Pour the filling into the baked crust and bake for 45 minutes, or until the center is set and doesn't jiggle when you gently shake the pie pan. Let cool on a wire rack. The pie can be refrigerated for up to 5 days.

Yield: one 10-inch (25 cm) pie

■ CRUSTLESS MAPLE-PECAN PIE

Soy-Free, Vegetarian

Using an entire tablespoon of sea salt sounds like a lot, but you'll wind up rinsing most of it away. Soaking the pecans in salted water overnight brings out their flavor and makes them even more buttery tasting. You might want to soak an extra handful to enjoy as a snack!

8 ounces (225 g) raw pecan halves	4 tablespoons (55 g) butter*
1 tablespoon (18 g) sea salt	3 eggs*
6 dates, pitted and chopped	2 teaspoons (10 ml) vanilla extract
¼ cup (60 ml) maple syrup	*See Notes on page 41

The night before, place the pecans and salt in a small bowl and add enough cold water to cover the nuts. Let sit on the counter overnight. The following day, rinse the nuts well and let drain. Preheat the oven to 225°F (105°C).

Spread the drained pecans on a rimmed baking sheet and bake for 15 minutes, or until the pecans are dry, brittle, and break apart easily. When they start to smell magnificently of roasting nuts, start checking them. (This is the most enchanting scent ever—not even baking bread can beat it!) While the pecans cool on a rack, increase the oven temperature to 350°F (180°C, or gas mark 4).

Place the dates, maple syrup, and butter in a small saucepan and heat over medium-low heat until the butter is melted. Raise the heat a notch or two until the mixture is gently bubbling. Let simmer for 3 minutes, then remove from the heat and whisk in the eggs and vanilla. Whisk in the pecans. Either break them into smaller bits with your hands or leave them as whole halves. I like the texture and look of the halves, so I do my best to keep them intact.

Pour the batter into an ungreased 9-inch (23 cm) glass pie pan. Bake for 30 minutes. Let the pie cool for 15 minutes before cutting into slices. Serve with whipped cream. Leftover pie can be refrigerated for up to 5 days. This makes a lovely breakfast!

Yield: one 9-inch (23 cm) pie

WHIPPED CREAM

½ cup (120 ml) whipping cream*, preferably not UHT
2 tablespoons (28 ml) maple syrup, optional
½ teaspoon vanilla extract, optional
*See Notes on page 41

Chill the beaters and bowl for at least 30 minutes in the fridge or 10 minutes in the freezer. Well-chilled equipment and ingredients are crucial, especially if you're using UHT cream. Pour the ingredient(s) into the chilled bowl and beat at high speed until the cream has become soft and fluffy. Refrigerate for up to 2 hours.

Yield: 1 cup (60 g)

■ PUMPKIN SPICE ICE CREAM

Nut-Free, Soy-Free, Vegetarian

Homemade ice cream tends to crystallize, but adding high-proof alcohol helps prevent that rock-solid hardness. If you'd rather skip the alcohol, let the ice cream sit at room temperature for at least 20 minutes before scooping and serving it. It's best to freeze ice cream in several small containers rather than one large one.

1 cup (235 ml) whole milk*
1 cup (245 g) canned pumpkin
4 egg yolks*
⅓ cup (80 ml) maple syrup
1 teaspoon ground cinnamon
½ teaspoon ground allspice

½ teaspoon ground ginger
¼ teaspoon ground cloves
1 shot (42 ml) unflavored vodka
   or rum, optional
1 teaspoon vanilla extract
See Notes on page 41

Place all the ingredients except the vodka and vanilla in a medium pot and whisk to combine. Heat over medium-low heat for 3 minutes, whisking occasionally. When tiny bubbles form, gently cook for another 5 minutes, whisking more often. Don't let it to come to a full simmer—that could overcook the egg yolks and make your ice cream chunky.

Remove from the heat and scoop into a cool bowl. Whisk in the vodka and vanilla. When the mixture is completely cool, place in an ice cream maker and freeze according to the manufacturer's instructions. Freeze churned ice cream in 2 pint-size (264 g) containers.

Yield: about 3 cups (396 g)

■ BLUEBERRY BUTTERMILK ICE CREAM

Nut-Free (use vanilla), Soy-Free, Vegetarian

Buttermilk makes lovely ice cream, especially when blended with berries. Be sure to use fresh berries—frozen berries contain too much water and will make the ice cream less creamy.

1 cup (235 ml) heavy cream*
1 cup (235 ml) buttermilk*
5 egg yolks*
¼ cup (85 g) honey, or more to taste
8 ounces (225 g) fresh blueberries

1 shot (42 ml) unflavored vodka or rum, optional
  (see headnote on page 164)
1 teaspoon almond or vanilla extract
See Notes on page 41

Place all the ingredients except the vodka and extract in a blender and blend until smooth. Transfer to a medium pot.

Heat the mixture over medium-low heat for 3 minutes, whisking occasionally. When tiny bubbles form, gently cook for another 5 minutes, whisking more often. Don't let it to come to a full simmer—that could overcook the egg yolks and make your ice cream chunky.

Remove from the heat and scoop into a cool bowl. Whisk in the vodka and extract. If you like, add more honey to taste. When the mixture is completely cool, place in an ice cream maker and freeze according to the manufacturer's instructions. Freeze churned ice cream in 2 pint-size (264 g) containers.

Yield: about 4 cups (528 g)

■ CHOCOLATE-COCONUT ICE CREAM

Dairy-Free, Soy-Free, Vegetarian

Here's proof that nondairy ice cream is just as good as conventional ice cream! In fact, you might be tempted to use whole coconut milk in other treats, too, like muffins and cakes. Go right ahead!

15 ounces (440 ml) whole coconut milk,
  preferably organic
5 egg yolks*
¼ cup (20 g) unsweetened cocoa powder*
¼ cup (60 ml) maple syrup
1 teaspoon vanilla extract

1 shot (42 ml) unflavored vodka or rum, optional
  (see headnote on page 164)
Toasted unsweetened flaked coconut for garnish,
  optional (see page 149)
See Notes on page 41

Place all the ingredients except the vodka and coconut flakes in a medium pot and whisk to combine.

Heat the mixture over medium-low heat for 3 minutes, whisking occasionally. When tiny bubbles form, gently cook for another 5 minutes, whisking more often. Don't let it to come to a full simmer—that could overcook the egg yolks and make your ice cream chunky.

Remove from the heat and scoop into a cool bowl. Whisk in the vodka. When the mixture is completely cool, place in an ice cream maker and freeze according to the manufacturer's instructions. Freeze churned ice cream in 2 pint-size (264 g) containers. Garnish with the toasted coconut just before serving.

Yield: about 3 cups (396 g)

■ BAKED BRIE WITH HOMEMADE MIXED-BERRY JAM

Nut-Free, Soy-Free, Egg-Free, Vegetarian

This dessert was inspired by a classic German dessert: baked Camembert cheese with Rote Grütze on top. You just can't go wrong when you combine warm, oozing cheese and sweet berry jam—especially when you make your own jam.

4 ounces (115 g) strawberries, tops trimmed*
4 ounces (115 g) blueberries
4 ounces (115 g) cranberries
¼ cup (60 ml) water

2 tablespoons (28 ml) maple syrup
One 8-ounce (225-g) wheel of Brie made with cow
   or goat's milk*
See Notes on page 41

Place the rinsed berries in a medium pot. Add the water and bring to a boil. Reduce the heat to medium and simmer for 10 minutes, then gently mash the berries with a potato masher. Add the maple syrup, reduce the heat to medium-low, and simmer for 45 minutes to 1 hour, or until the berries have thickened. You'll have about 1 ¼ cups (400 g) jam.

Preheat the oven to 325°F (170°C, or gas mark 3). Line an 8 x 8-inch (20 x 20 cm) pan with parchment paper and place the wheel of Brie in the center of it. Pour the jam onto the Brie and bake for 10 to 15 minutes or until the Brie is melting. Remove from the oven and let cool slightly before enjoying. This dessert is best eaten with spoons!

Yield: 4 servings

▶ MODERN-DAY SYLLABUBS
Nut-Free, Soy-Free, Egg-Free, Vegetarian

If you like, place the cloves, cinnamon stick, and vanilla bean in a muslin teabag or a corner of cheesecloth tied shut with an undyed cotton string. Then they'll be easier to remove before serving.

Juice and zest of 2 large oranges,
  plus juice of 2 additional oranges*
¼ cup (60 ml) water
1 tablespoon (15 ml) maple syrup, or more to taste
10 whole cloves
1 cinnamon stick

1 vanilla bean, slit lengthwise with
  the tip of a sharp knife
2 cups (120 g) whipped cream* (see page 163)
Dry red wine or dry hard cider, for drizzling
See Notes on page 41

Place the orange juice and zest in a medium pot. Add the water, syrup, spices, and vanilla bean. Bring to a boil over medium heat, then reduce the heat to low. Simmer uncovered for 40 minutes, stirring occasionally, or until the mixture has reduced by half. Remove the spices and vanilla bean. If you'd like the syrup to be sweeter, add more maple syrup to taste. Remove from the heat.

For a melting effect, serve the syrup warm; for an airy effect, refrigerate the syrup to chill it before serving. To make each dessert, place ½ cup (30 g) whipped cream in 4 small bowls. Ladle the spiced orange syrup over the freshly whipped cream, drizzle with the wine, and serve promptly.

Yield: 4 servings

■ SAUTÉED PINEAPPLE & BANANA WITH TOASTED COCONUT
Dairy-Free (use coconut oil), Soy-Free, Egg-Free, Vegetarian, 20 minutes or less

Ripe pineapples and bananas caramelize without any additional sugar. Look for pineapples that are yellowed, fragrant, and heavy (but without any soft spots or blemishes), and choose bananas that are well spotted but not blackened.

¼ cup (22 g) unsweetened flaked coconut
Unrefined coconut oil or butter, for cooking
½ small ripe pineapple, peeled, cored, and
  cut into bite-size chunks

2 large ripe peeled bananas, peeled and cut into ½-inch
  (1.3 cm) rounds

Heat the coconut in a medium skillet over medium heat. Toast for 5 minutes, stirring occasionally, or until the coconut is fragrant and turning light brown. Immediately transfer the coconut to a plate.

In a large skillet, melt a spoonful of coconut oil or generous pat of butter over medium heat. Add the pineapple and banana and cook, stirring occasionally, for 5 minutes, or until the fruit is turning golden brown around the edges.

Divide the fruit into 4 portions and sprinkle each with the toasted coconut before serving. Any leftovers can be refrigerated and puréed into a smoothie with whole coconut milk the next day.

Yield: 4 servings

◼ WINE GLASS CHOCOLATE & FRUIT PARFAITS

Soy-Free, Egg-Free, Vegetarian, 20 minutes or less

Dutch-process cocoa powder is cocoa powder that's been treated with an alkali to tone down the cocoa's natural acidity. Dutchman Coenraad Johannes van Houten came up with the technique back in the 1800s, and it's been used ever since. I object! Why un-chocolate chocolate? Its acidity is part of its inherent appeal, plus "natural" (that is, non-alkalized) cocoa powder boasts a richer aroma and a lighter, slightly reddish color.

For the toppings:
16 strawberries, tops trimmed*
2 tablespoons (28 ml) balsamic vinegar
Handful of sliced almonds, chopped pecans, or
    chopped walnuts, toasted (see page 112)
2 cups (120 g) sweetened whipped cream* (see page 163)

For the chocolate layer:
½ cup (40 g) unsweetened cocoa powder*
¼ cup (60 ml) maple syrup
2 cups (460 g) plain whole-milk Greek yogurt*
See Notes on page 41

To make the toppings: Slice the strawberries, place in a bowl, and toss with the balsamic vinegar. Let soak while you toast the nuts and whip the cream. Drain the strawberries just before assembling the parfaits.

To make the chocolate layer: Stir the cocoa powder and maple syrup into the yogurt with a small whisk, mixing until smooth.

To assemble the parfaits, have 4 pretty wine glasses ready. Working with one glass at a time, scoop ¼ cup (60 g) chocolate yogurt into each glass. Cover with a layer of strawberries, then add another ¼ cup (60 g) chocolate yogurt and another layer of strawberries. Finish by topping each parfait with ½ cup (30 g) whipped cream and a sprinkling of toasted nuts.

Yield: 4 servings

ACKNOWLEDGMENTS

This book is for my parents, especially my mom. She's the most creative, confident, and efficient cook I know—and wow, can she plate a dish! No matter her medium (edibles, textiles, paints, flowers), she's a true artist. I'd also like to thank my many friends who've supported my I-want-to-be-an-author dreams over the years. Thank you for never doubting me, not even when the rejection slips were piling up. To my culinary friends who've been sampling my creations over the years, thank you for helping me fine-tune the recipes and ideas in this book. Here's to many more meals to come!

Many thanks to the publishing professionals in my life for transforming my literary/culinary aspirations into a concrete book. Sally Ekus and Lisa Ekus, you are the best agents I can imagine! You just "get" me—your support has meant more than I can say in words. Amanda, you are an amazing editor! Your guidance has been a soothing blend of adjusting, polishing, and making this book blossom. A cookbook isn't an easy thing to create, but having a supportive editor makes the process indescribably more doable.

And then there's the Tasteful Twelve, who enthusiastically tested recipes for this book and offered insightful and invaluable feedback. The Twelve include Jill (she used to be a chicken-and-potatoes girl, but now she's willing to try whatever I concoct), Tanya (when she found out she was celiac, she became my chief inspiration for exploring the gluten-free world), Michael and André (their unwavering support for my quality-over-quantity ideas has encouraged me to continually upgrade my ingredients and recipes), Karen G. (I hope that one day I have a kitchen half as gorgeous as hers!), Pauline (a fellow food coach who took me to transcendent food destinations when I visited her San Francisco stomping grounds), Lauryn (she's just as fervent about grass-fed animal products as I am, plus her pantry is stocked with whole-grain everything), Karen M. (even with a broken arm, she loves to get her hands dirty in the kitchen), Susan (if I ever have a question about sushi, Asian cuisine, Californian ingredients, or barbecueing, I know who to ask!), Adam (when you want to know whether a recipe works in every aspect, you give that recipe to an engineer with a Ph.D. in physics), Debbie (a committed gluten-free gal with freshly hunted venison in her freezer and outrageously oversized veggies in her garden), Jennifer (fellow fan of the written word and salsa dancing, plus she can identify obscure Hungarian spirits at a glance in a dimly lit bar), and Jennie (a kindred spirit who also loves to explore recipes, ingredients, and fun kitchen gadgets like the Almighty Vitamix). And—of course!—my mom, who made the Tasteful Twelve a lucky baker's dozen. Thanks again for everything you've taught me over the years!

ABOUT THE AUTHOR

Culinary speaker, cooking instructor, and recipe developer Lisa Howard loves to share her joy of food with others. Through her recipes and classes, she helps her fellow eaters understand where to find delicious ingredients, why those ingredients are just as nutritious as they are delicious, and how to prepare them. Stop by her virtual kitchen at www.theculturedcook.com to check out more recipes and healthy tips. And if you happen to be in Metro Detroit, look for her wherever a Latin band is playing—when she's not in the kitchen, she's usually salsa dancing!

INDEX

acorn nuts, 23
all-purpose flour, 17
almonds
    Almond Sponge Cake with Chocolate
        Ganache Frosting, 143
    Almond-Dusted Crab Cakes, 91
    flour, 22, 91
    Gingersnaps with Teff & Almond, 156
    Moroccan Almond & Lamb Meatballs,
        126
amaranth, 86
    Amaranth Pizza Muffins, 120
    flour, 23
animal products, 41
apples
    Apple Pie with Nut & Oat Crust, 160
    Pumpkin-Maple Dip with Apples &
        Pears, 133
    Zucchini, Apple, & Pecan Quick Bread
        with Teff Flour, 46
arrowroot, 24
Artichoke Dip, White Bean &, 117
Asian Dressing, 82
autoimmune disorders, 8, 12, 13
avocado
    Crab, Avocado & Mango Lettuce Wraps
        with Dijon Dressing, 57
    Cumin-Scented Guacamole, 131
    Shrimp Scramble with Chopped
        Avocado & Mango, 52

B vitamins, 17, 18
bacon
    Bacon, Onion & Spinach Frittata, 55
    Open-Faced BLT on a Savory Pancake,
        69
    Paella with Shrimp & Bacon, 87
baked goods, 18, 20
Baked Mac 'N' Cheese Starring Brown Rice
    Pasta, 97
baking ingredients, 41
baking powder, 39, 41
baking soda, 39
baking techniques, 40
bananas
    Banana-Ginger Quick Bread with
        Chopped Macadamias, 47
    Sautéed Pineapple & Banana with
        Toasted Coconut, 168
bar cookies, 36
barley, 10, 11, 15
beans. See black beans; green beans; lentils;
    white beans
beer, 14, 37
Berber-Dusted Popcorn, 113
beriberi, 17
beverages

Homemade Sodas, 137
    Hot Chocolate, 138
biscotti, 36
    Chocolate- and Pine-Nut-Studded
        Biscotti, 158
biscuits, 37
black beans
    flour, 24
    Noodle-Free Mexican Lasagna, 94
    Savory Salsa-and-Black Bean
        Cornbread, 121
    South-of-the-Border Quinoa Bowl, 86
blueberries
    Baked Brie with Homemade Mixed-
        Berry Jam, 166
    Blueberry Buttermilk Ice Cream, 165
    Blueberry-Buckwheat Yogurt Muffins,
        45
BPA, 41
Brazil nut flour, 22
bread crumbs, 37
bread flour, 10
breads, 37
brie
    Baked Brie with Homemade Mixed-
        Berry Jam, 166
    Brie & Pear Quesadillas, 68
broths, 14
brown rice pasta, 97
brown rice syrup, 31
Brownies, Ultra-Dark Oat & Date, 151
Bruschetta, Baked Mochi, 125
Brussels Sprout "Truffles," Savory, 125
buckwheat, 23, 121
    Blueberry-Buckwheat Yogurt Muffins,
        45
    Buckwheat Tabbouleh, 85
bulgur, 10
butter, 27, 33
buttermilk, 27–28
    Blueberry Buttermilk Ice Cream, 165
    Savory Herbed Buttermilk-Potato
        Waffles, 50
Butternut Squash Soup, Roasted, 109

Cabbage Romaine Boats, Korean-Style
    Pork &, 60
Caesar Salad, Mom's, 80
cake flour, 10
cakes, 36
    Almond Sponge Cake with Chocolate
        Ganache Frosting, 143
    Chocolate Angel Food Cake with
        Smashed Raspberry Glaze, 147
    Five-Minute Chestnut Fudge Cake, 148
    Orange-Coconut Cake, 149
    Peach-Swirled Cheesecake, 141
    Spiced Mesquite & Sorghum Coffee
        Cake, 150
    Vanilla Chiffon Cake with Fresh

Strawberries & Whipped Cream, 145
canned goods, 41
carob powder, 25
Cayenne Parmesan Popcorn, 113
celiac disease, 8, 12, 15
cereals, 14, 37
    DIY Whole-Grain Cereal, 43
chayote, 107
cheese, 28, 33
    Baked Brie with Homemade Mixed-
        Berry Jam, 166
    Baked Mac 'N' Cheese Starring Brown
        Rice Pasta, 97
    Brie & Pear Quesadillas, 68
    Buttery Cheddar-Sage Crackers, 136
    Cornbread Panzanella with Mozzarella
        Pearls, 77
    Free-Form Goat Cheese, Millet &
        Walnut Scones with Pears, 48
    Goat Cheese, Fig & Caramelized Onion
        Pizza, 70
    Grilled Polenta Melts, 114
    Moroccan Quesadillas, 66
    Noodle-Free Mexican Lasagna, 94
    Pear, Walnut & Gorgonzola Salad, 73
    Salty-Sweet Halloumi & Grape Salad,
        80
    Tomato-Basil Soup with White Beans &
        Feta, 104
cheesecakes, 37
    Peach-Swirled Cheesecake, 141
chestnut
    Chestnut Snickerdoodles with Pine Nuts,
        155
    Five-Minute Chestnut Fudge Cake, 148
    flour, 22
chia seeds, 23
chicken
    Moroccan Millet Couscous with
        Chicken, Olives & Lemon, 83
    Savory Chickpea Crepes with Curried
        Chicken, 62
    (Whole-Grain) Breaded Chicken Fingers
        with Mustard Dip, 92
chickpeas
    Break-the-Fast Chickpea & Lamb
        Harira, 102
    Collard-Wrapped Tuna & Hummus
        Rolls, 59
    Crispy Pan-Fried Chickpeas, 119
    flour, 24
    Hummus Three Ways: Red Pepper,
        Cilantro & Roasted Eggplant, 116
    Savory Chickpea Crepes with Curried
        Chicken, 62
Chili Sauce, Spicy, 129
chips, 37
chocolate
    Chocolate- and Pine-Nut-Studded
        Biscotti, 158